A GUIDE TO THE AFFORDABLE CARE ACT FOR LOCAL GOVERNMENT EMPLOYERS

DIANE M. JUFFRAS 2016

UNC
SCHOOL OF GOVERNMENT

The School of Government at the University of North Carolina at Chapel Hill works to improve the lives of North Carolinians by engaging in practical scholarship that helps public officials and citizens understand and improve state and local government. Established in 1931 as the Institute of Government, the School provides educational, advisory, and research services for state and local governments. The School of Government is also home to a nationally ranked Master of Public Administration program, the North Carolina Judicial College, and specialized centers focused on community and economic development, information technology, and environmental finance.

As the largest university-based local government training, advisory, and research organization in the United States, the School of Government offers up to 200 courses, webinars, and specialized conferences for more than 12,000 public officials each year. In addition, faculty members annually publish approximately 50 books, manuals, reports, articles, bulletins, and other print and online content related to state and local government. The School also produces the *Daily Bulletin Online* each day the General Assembly is in session, reporting on activities for members of the legislature and others who need to follow the course of legislation.

Operating support for the School of Government's programs and activities comes from many sources, including state appropriations, local government membership dues, private contributions, publication sales, course fees, and service contracts.

Visit sog.unc.edu or call 919.966.5381 for more information on the School's courses, publications, programs, and services.

Michael R. Smith, DEAN
Thomas H. Thornburg, SENIOR ASSOCIATE DEAN
Frayda S. Bluestein, ASSOCIATE DEAN FOR FACULTY DEVELOPMENT
Johnny Burleson, ASSOCIATE DEAN FOR DEVELOPMENT
Michael Vollmer, ASSOCIATE DEAN FOR ADMINISTRATION
Linda H. Weiner, ASSOCIATE DEAN FOR OPERATIONS
Janet Holston, DIRECTOR OF STRATEGY AND INNOVATION

FACULTY

Whitney Afonso	Cheryl Daniels Howell	David W. Owens
Trey Allen	Jeffrey A. Hughes	LaToya B. Powell
Gregory S. Allison	Willow S. Jacobson	William C. Rivenbark
David N. Ammons	Robert P. Joyce	Dale J. Roenigk
Ann M. Anderson	Diane M. Juffras	John Rubin
Maureen Berner	Dona G. Lewandowski	Jessica Smith
Mark F. Botts	Adam Lovelady	Meredith Smith
Anita R. Brown-Graham	James M. Markham	Carl W. Stenberg III
Peg Carlson	Christopher B. McLaughlin	John B. Stephens
Leisha DeHart-Davis	Kara A. Millonzi	Charles Szypszak
Shea Riggsbee Denning	Jill D. Moore	Shannon H. Tufts
Sara DePasquale	Jonathan Q. Morgan	Vaughn Mamlin Upshaw
James C. Drennan	Ricardo S. Morse	Aimee N. Wall
Richard D. Ducker	C. Tyler Mulligan	Jeffrey B. Welty
Norma Houston	Kimberly L. Nelson	Richard B. Whisnant

ISBN 978-1-56011-876-3

Contents

PART 2

Determining Who Is a Covered Employer

Part 1

Introduction to the Affordable Care Act (ACA) and the Employer Mandate

The Affordable Care Act was enacted in 2010 to reduce the cost of health care, make health care affordable and accessible to all Americans, and improve the quality of health care. To accomplish these goals, the ACA imposed new requirements on health insurers, individual consumers (patients), and employers, who provide the majority of Americans below the age of 65 with their access to health care through group health plans.[1] The ACA is, not surprisingly, a complicated law with complicated regulations. These regulations have been issued by no fewer than three federal agencies—the Department of the Treasury (primarily through the Internal Revenue Service (IRS)), the Department of Labor (primarily through the Employment Benefits Security Administration), and the Department of Health and Human Services. While this book is about the requirements the ACA places on employers, requirements commonly known as the employer mandate, the interlocking nature of the employer mandate, marketplace reforms imposed on insurers,

---

1. *See, e.g.,* The Henry J. Kaiser Family Foundation, *The Uninsured: A Primer 2013–1: How Did Most Americans Obtain Health Insurance in 2012?* Kaiser Family Foundation Report (November 14, 2013), http://kff.org/report-section/the-uninsured-a-primer-2013-1-how-did-most-americans-obtain-health-insurance-in-2012/; Elizabeth Mendes, *Fewer Americans Getting Health Insurance from Employer: Medicare, Medicaid, and Military or Veterans' Insurance Inching Higher,* report on results of Gallup Poll (February 22, 2013), http://www.gallup.com/poll/160676/fewer-americans-getting-health-insurance-employer.aspx.

and the requirements placed on individuals requires a brief explanation of all three facets of the law.

The Employer Mandate

The requirements the ACA places on employers are known as the "employer mandate."[2] The employer mandate requires that employers with 50 or more employees[3] offer health insurance coverage that is affordable and provides minimum value to 95% of their full-time employees and their dependents or face penalties. Employers who have fewer than 50 employees are not subject to the employer mandate.

There are two kinds of penalties. The first is the no-coverage penalty. If an employer offers coverage to fewer than 95% of its full-time employees, it may be liable for the no-coverage penalty. The no-coverage penalty applies only when at least one employee receives a tax credit from the U.S. government to help pay for the cost of health insurance premiums for coverage acquired on the exchanges set up under the ACA. The IRS will know which individuals have received such a tax credit and, because of ACA reporting requirements, it will know which of those individuals is an employee of a particular employer. The no-coverage penalty is slightly more than 1/12 of $2,000 per month for each employee who should have been offered coverage but was not.

Even if an employer offers coverage to 95% of its employees, it can be liable for a second possible penalty, the inadequate-coverage penalty. This penalty is assessed when an employer offers coverage that is either not "affordable" or does not provide "minimum value." To be affordable with respect to any particular employee, the employee's required contribution toward the cost of self-only coverage must not exceed approximately 9.5% of the employee's household income for the year. To provide minimum value, a health insurance plan must cover at least 60% of the total cost of benefits the plan could objectively be expected to incur if it served a statistically standard population. This is a complicated calculation. Both the requirements that a plan be

---

2. The federal government agencies tasked with implementing the ACA generally refer to these as the "employer shared-responsibility" provisions. In the media, they are sometimes referred to as "pay-or-play" provisions.

3. Technically, the threshold is 50 or more full-time equivalents. See pages 37–38.

affordable and that it offer minimum value are discussed in greater detail on pages 21–32. Like the no-coverage penalty, the inadequate-coverage penalty is assessed only when at least one employee receives a tax credit to help pay for health insurance premiums for coverage purchased on the exchanges set up under the ACA.

The inadequate-coverage penalty is slightly more than 1/12 of $3,000 each month for every employee who receives the premium tax credit. There is a cap on the amount of the inadequate-coverage penalty designed to ensure that an employer who offers coverage (although inadequate or below minimum value) will never pay a greater penalty than an employer who offers no coverage at all.

The Individual Mandate

In addition to imposing the employer mandate on large employers, the ACA also requires virtually all individuals to secure health insurance that provides minimum essential coverage (MEC), qualify for a health coverage exemption, or pay a penalty (or, as the IRS would have it, make an individual shared-responsibility payment). That's the "individual mandate." To help individuals meet this mandate, the federal government has set up online health insurance exchanges (the "Exchange" or "Exchanges") designed to assist individuals who do not get health insurance coverage through their employment to purchase it.

An employee who gets coverage through an employer-sponsored health plan that satisfies the employer mandate has, by definition, minimum essential coverage or MEC and is therefore meeting the employee's own individual-mandate obligation. When individuals cannot afford the coverage offered through their or their family member's employer for any or all months, they are exempt from the individual mandate. Whether coverage is affordable is an objective judgment: an individual cannot afford coverage if the individual's required contribution for minimum essential coverage exceeds 8% (as indexed annually) of the individual's household income.[4]

---

4. *See* 26 U.S.C. § 5000A(e)(1) and 26 C.F.R. § 1.5000A-3(e).

Shared Responsibility

Together, the employer mandate and the individual mandate make up what the ACA calls "shared responsibility" for ensuring that individuals have health insurance coverage—an obligation that rests both with individuals and with employers that have at least 50 employees.

The Premium Tax Credit and the Employer-Mandate Reporting Requirements

Employers can be liable for the no-coverage or inadequate-coverage penalty only if at least one employee receives a premium tax credit. Here's how that works. When an employee cannot afford an employer's offer of health insurance coverage whether for him- or herself or for the employee's dependents, the employee's only remaining option for health insurance is generally to purchase an individual or family policy through the state's online health care exchange or "Marketplace" or in the federally operated online Marketplace. North Carolina, for example, does not operate a health insurance marketplace and individuals must access the North Carolina Marketplace through the federal government's Healthcare.gov website.[5] Maryland, on the other hand, is an example of a state that has created its own exchange or marketplace, the Maryland Health Connection. Residents of Maryland would access that state's marketplace directly and not through Healthcare.gov.[6]

To be eligible for a premium tax credit, the employee's household income must be between 100% and 400% of the federal poverty level for the employee's family size.[7] Under the premium tax credit program, the federal government pays a portion of the premium directly to the insurer or credits or refunds the amount of the credit on the employee's federal tax return. The

---

5. Go to https://www.healthcare.gov/get-coverage/.

6. Go to https://www.marylandhealthconnection.gov/.

7. According to the IRS, household income would have been at least 100% but no more than 400% of the federal poverty line in 2015 at the following levels:

$11,670 (100%) up to $46,680 (400%) for one individual
$15,730 (100%) up to $62,920 (400%) for a family of two
$23,850 (100%) up to $95,400 (400%) for a family of four

See Internal Revenue Service, Questions and Answers on the Premium Tax Credit, https://www.irs.gov/affordable-care-act/individuals-and-families/questions-and-answers-on-the-premium-tax-credit. Individuals and families with income less than the federal poverty line likely will qualify for health insurance coverage through Medicaid.

size of the premium tax credit is based on a sliding scale. Those who have a lower income get a larger credit.

The employer of an individual who obtains health insurance coverage through a marketplace or exchange and receives a premium tax credit is subject to either a no-coverage penalty or an inadequate-coverage penalty.

The IRS must keep track of which employers offer affordable coverage that provides minimum value to their employees and which individuals purchase coverage through an exchange using a premium tax credit. It does this by requiring covered employers, insurers, and the individual exchanges to file information reports with the IRS every year through a series of complicated forms.

Employers with 50 or more full-time equivalent employees (FTEs) give IRS Form 1095-C to each employee to whom they have offered coverage, whether or not the employee has accepted the offer. Form 1095-C asks for information about the premium amounts that employees must contribute for coverage under the employer plan for each month of the year, whether or not the employee and any dependents were enrolled in coverage. It also asks for information about employees who were not offered coverage. Employers must then submit copies of all of the Forms 1095-C they have given to their employees to the IRS along with a transmittal summary sheet, Form 1094-C, which provides the IRS aggregate data about offers of health coverage. The information supplied on Forms 1094-C and 1095-C helps the IRS track compliance with the employer and individual mandates.

Employer health plans may be fully insured or self-insured. In a fully insured plan, the employer pays an insurance company to take the risk of and legal responsibility for uncertain health care costs. In a self-insured plan, the employer uses its own funds to provide health benefits to its employees. In doing so, the employer assumes the risk of and legal responsibility for uncertain health care costs. Self-insured employers have additional reporting responsibilities not shared by fully insured employers. That is because the ACA imposes extra reporting requirements on health insurers, primarily to assist in assessing compliance with the individual mandate, and self-insured employers are treated as health insurers. This extra information is reported on a separate form, Form 1095-B. Employers who offer fully insured plans—that is, plans for which they pay the insurance company monthly premiums in return for which the insurance company pays claims to doctors and other health care professionals and entities—do not have to file Form 1095-B. The insurance company with which they have contracted will complete and file Forms 1095-B and the accompanying summary transmittal form, Form 1094-B. But self-insured employers *are* the insurance company for ACA reporting purposes, even if the employer contracts with a third-party administrator to manage the plan's day-to-day operations. Thus self-insured employers must supply the information the IRS requests on both sets of forms, Forms 1095-C and transmittal Form 1094-C and Forms 1095-B and transmittal Form 1094-B.

Fortunately for self-insured employers, the IRS has foreseen this difficulty and provided a section (Part III) on Form 1095-C in which self-insured employers may provide the information otherwise required by Form 1095-B.

As mentioned above, the health care exchanges must also furnish information to the IRS to assist it in assessing who is entitled to a premium tax credit. The information required of the exchanges need not concern us here.[8]

Self-Insured Small Employer Reporting Requirements

Small employers who are self-insured—that is, employers with fewer than 50 FTEs who are exempt from the employer mandate—still must send completed Forms 1095-B to their employees and to the IRS, along with transmittal summary Form 1094-B, in their role as insurers.

Features the ACA Requires All Employer Plans to Offer

The employer mandate was part of the ACA when it was signed into law in 2010, but it has been among the last of the Act's provisions to be implemented. Other provisions of the ACA became effective beginning in 2011. Among the earlier provisions implemented were those setting forth new standards for group health insurance plans. Thus, with the employer mandate now effective, covered employers not only have to offer health insurance to their full-time employees, but they must also offer health insurance that meets the ACA's substantive plan requirements.

---

8. *See* 26 U.S.C. § 36B(f)(3) and 26 C.F.R. § 1.36B-5(c) for details about Exchange reporting requirements.

The regulations governing what the ACA calls "essential health benefits," which must be included in most plans, apply to health insurance issuers rather than employers. So employers purchasing health insurance products from health insurance companies and self-insured employers contracting with health insurance consultants to design their plans will not need to know the substantive requirements health plans must meet. They may, however, find it helpful to understand what must be included in the health insurance plans from which they will make their choices and what is optional.

Some requirements apply only to small employers (those purchasing in the ACA's "small group market," defined as employers with 50 or fewer employees),[9] and some requirements do not apply to grandfathered plans (plans in existence as of 2010 whose coverage has remained the same). These will be discussed later.

No-Cost Coverage of Preventative Care and Immunizations

All large and small employer plans, both insured and self-insured, must provide preventative care and immunizations free of charge.[10] No co-payments, co-insurance, or deductibles may be assessed for these services. The text of the ACA itself and ACA regulations set forth the specific preventative health services and immunizations plans must provide at no-cost.[11] Only grandfathered plans (see below, page 16) may impose cost-sharing charges for these services.[12]

Emergency Care Cost-Sharing the Same In-Network and Out-of-Network

The ACA permits employers to offer health plans that have a preferred network of providers, but plans must cover emergency services on the same basis whether the hospital and providers are in-network or out-of-network.[13] Cost-sharing for emergency services must be the same for both in-network

---

9. *See* 42 U.S.C. § 18024(b)(2).

10. *See* 29 C.F.R. § 2590.715-2713.

11. *See* 42 U.S.C. § 300gg–13(a); 29 C.F.R. § 2590.715-2713(a)(1). *See also* U.S. Department of Labor, *FAQs about Affordable Care Act Implementation (Part XXVI)* (May 11, 2015) (hereinafter *FAQs about Affordable Care Act Implementation (Part XXVI)*), www.dol.gov/EBSA/faqs/faq-aca26.html.

12. Employer-sponsored group health plans that were in effect on March 23, 2010, and have provided continuous coverage ever since are considered "grandfathered" plans. *See* 42 U.S.C. § 18011; 29 C.F.R. § 2590.715-2713(d); 45 C.F.R. § 147.140(c)(1).

13. *See* 45 C.F.R. § 156.130(g); 45 C.F.R. § 147.138(b).

and out-of-network providers, except that the plan may charge a participant any charges the plan incurs as a result of a difference between the in-network rate and the rate out-of-network providers may charge.[14] Grandfathered plans are not subject to this requirement.

Limits on Overall Employee Cost-Sharing

No essential health benefit may be subject to a lifetime or annual limit. This rule applies both to small employer health plans (50 or fewer employees), which must offer coverage of all ten essential health benefits, and to large employer plans, self-insured plans, and grandfathered plans that offer any of the ten essential health benefits.[15]

Additionally, the ACA limits the amount an employer's health plan may require employees to contribute out-of-pocket toward health care costs for essential health benefits. This limitation applies to employers subject to the employer mandate, but not to grandfathered plans (freedom from this limitation is one of the major differences between grandfathered and non-grandfathered plans).[16] Out-of-pocket costs subject to this limitation include deductibles, co-insurance, co-payments, and similar charges. Premiums, costs of treatment from non-network providers that exceed what the plan will pay, and spending for non-covered services are not included in the limit on out-of-pocket expenses.[17] The limits for out-of-pocket payments for deductibles, co-insurance, copays, and other expenditures for calendar year 2017 are $7,150 for individuals and $14,300 for families.[18] These figures are adjusted annually for inflation.[19]

---

14. *See* 45 C.F.R. §§ 147.138(b)(3)(i) and (ii).

15. *See* U.S. Department of Labor, *FAQs about Affordable Care Act Implementation (Part XXVII)* (May 15, 2015) (hereinafter *FAQs about Affordable Care Act Implementation (Part XXVII)*), www.dol.gov/EBSA/faqs/faq-aca27.html.

16. *See* pages 13–20 for more information about grandfathered plans.

17. *See* 45 C.F.R. § 155.20 defining *cost-sharing*.

18. *See* 80 Fed. Reg. 75488, 75547 (December 2, 2015).

19. The maximum annual limit on an employee's share of the cost of health care is determined by reference to the annual premium adjustment percentage. The annual premium adjustment percentage is the percentage by which the average per capita premium for health insurance coverage for the preceding calendar year exceeds the average per capita premium for health insurance for 2013. The U.S. Department of Health and Human Services (HHS) publishes the premium adjustment percentage and the maximum annual limitation on cost-sharing annually in its Notice of Benefit and Payment Parameters. For 2016, HHS determined the premium adjustment percentage

What Counts toward the Out-of-Pocket Maximum?

Yes	No
Deductibles	Premiums
Co-payments	Non-essential health benefits
Emergency care	Essential health benefits outside plan's network

No Pre-existing Coverage Exclusions

The ACA provides that coverage offered by group health plans may not be limited or denied because of a person's pre-existing health condition.[20] This provision applies to all plans, including self-insured and grandfathered plans.[21] This absolute prohibition against the exclusion of pre-existing conditions is an important change from prior practice. Before the ACA, employees who changed jobs and had to enroll in their new employer's health insurance coverage had to show "prior creditable coverage" under another health plan for a pre-existing condition to be covered by the new employer's plan. Human resources departments no longer have to issue certificates of creditable coverage to employees leaving an employer, nor do they have to ask new employees with existing conditions for copies of their certificates of creditable coverage.

No Enrollment Waiting Periods Longer than 90 Days

The ACA allows employers to require a waiting period of no more than 90 days before otherwise eligible employees and their dependents begin coverage under the employer's group health plan. The concept of "otherwise eligible" refers to requirements the employer may impose for an employee to participate in the employer's health insurance plan, such as being in a particular job classification (for example, all administrative or management employees, or all public safety employees), working a certain number of hours per week, satisfying all licensure requirements for the position, or

---

to be 8.316047520. *See* 26 C.F.R. § 54.4980H; 80 Fed. Reg. 10750, 10825 (February 27, 2015). For 2017, the set premium adjustment percentage is approximately 13%. *See* 81 Fed. Reg. 12203 (March 8, 2016).

20. *See* 45 C.F.R. § 147.108(a).

21. *See* 45 C.F.R. § 147.108(b)(3).

completing a probationary or orientation period.[22] Once a new employee satisfies all of the requirements to participate in the health plan, the employee cannot be required to wait more than 90 calendar days (including weekends and holidays) after the date upon which the employee satisfies the prerequisites to enroll in the health plan.[23] Grandfathered plans are also subject to this requirement.[24]

Mandatory Coverage for Children up to Age 26

The ACA requires employer-sponsored group health plans to offer dependent coverage or face a penalty. It does not, however, require plans to offer spousal coverage. The ACA regulations define *dependent* for the purpose of eligibility for health plan coverage only in terms of the relationship of parent and child. Definitions of dependent found elsewhere in the Internal Revenue Code or in other employee benefits legislation do not apply here. Thus, the dependent coverage mandate extends not only to children who are full-time students, but also to married children and those who are financially independent.[25]

Dependent coverage must be available until the child turns 26 years of age.[26] When a child turns 26 and is no longer eligible for coverage under a parent's plan, the child's loss of coverage is treated as a COBRA qualifying event that allows for continuation coverage up to 18 months.[27] These rules apply equally to grandfathered health plans.[28]

The definition of *dependent* expressly excludes stepchildren and foster children from its scope. Nevertheless, the IRS has indicated that while employers do not have to offer coverage of stepchildren or foster children, if

---

22. *See* below, Part 3, page 67.

23. *See* 26 C.F.R. §§ 54.9815-2708(a)–(c); 29 C.F.R. §§ 2590.715-2708(a)–(c); 45 C.F.R. §§ 147.116(a)–(c).

24. *See* 26 C.F.R. § 54.9815-2708(i); 29 C.F.R. § 2590.715-2708(i); 45 C.F.R. § 147.116(i).

25. *See* 26 C.F.R. § 54.9815-2714T(b); 29 C.F.R. § 2590.715-2714(b); 45 C.F.R. § 147.120(b).

26. *See* 42 U.S.C. § 300gg-14(a); 26 C.F.R. § 54.9815-2714T(a)(1); 29 C.F.R. § 2590.715-2714(a)(1); 45 C.F.R. § 147.120(a)(1).

27. *See* 42 U.S.C. §§ 300bb-2 and 300bb-3. Dependent children who experience a second COBRA qualifying event during the first 18 months of continuation coverage may be entitled to up to 36 months of coverage.

28. *See* 26 C.F.R. § 54.9815-2714T(g)(2); 29 C.F.R. § 2590.715-2714(g)(2); 45 C.F.R. § 147.120(g)(2).

they do they must treat stepchildren and foster children the same as biological children, including offering coverage until age 26.[29]

Employers are not required to contribute any amount whatsoever to the cost of a dependent child's health insurance, even if they pay all or part of the employee's health insurance premium. The only requirement is that an employer-sponsored plan offer dependent coverage (and it is usually at the employee's own cost) until an employee's dependents reach age 26.[30]

No Rescission of Coverage

The Affordable Care Act prohibits group health plans and health insurance issuers offering group or individual health insurance coverage from rescinding coverage except in the case of fraud or intentional misrepresentation of material fact.[31] A study conducted prior to the passage of the ACA found that during the period 2004–2008, rescissions averaged 1.46 per thousand policies in force.[32] Under the ACA, there will be many fewer rescissions. In the past, coverage was often rescinded when insurance companies did not review medical histories when applications were submitted but then investigated policyholders when they became sick and filed expensive claims. If the insurance company found discrepancies, omissions, or misrepresentations, it generally rescinded the policies, returned the premiums, and refused payment for medical services. This is no longer permitted unless the employee/policyholder has intentionally withheld or mischaracterized information provided to the insurer.

---

29. There is limited guidance other than the interim final rule on coverage of children up to age 26. *See* U.S. Department of Labor, *Young Adults and the Affordable Care Act: Protecting Young Adults and Eliminating Burdens on Businesses and Families FAQs* (hereinafter *Young Adults and the Affordable Care Act*), http://www.dol.gov/ebsa/faqs/faq-dependentcoverage.html; U.S. Department of Health and Human Services, Centers for Medicare and Medicaid Services, *Questions and Answers on Enrollment of Children under 19 under the New Policy That Prohibits Pre-existing Condition Exclusions* (hereinafter *Questions and Answers on Enrollment of Children under 19*), http://www.cms.gov/CCIIO/Resources/Files/factsheet.html.

30. As of the publication date of this book, there is only limited guidance, including an interim final rule, on coverage of children up to age 26. *See Young Adults and the Affordable Care Act; Questions and Answers on Enrollment of Children under 19.*

31. *See* 42 U.S.C. § 300gg-12.

32. *See NAIC Rescission Data Call*, December 17, 2009, at 1, cited in Internal Revenue Bulletin 2010-32 (August 9, 2010), at note 21.

Enhanced Claims Review Process

Under the ACA, plans must provide an internal claims process, provide appropriate notice to employees, allow employees to review their files and present evidence and testimony as part of the review process, and allow all employees to receive continued coverage during the appeals process.[33] These requirements do not apply to grandfathered plans.[34]

Repeal of Automatic Enrollment for Larger Employers

As originally enacted, the ACA required employers with 200 or more employees to enroll employees in their group health plan automatically. In the Bipartisan Budget Act of 2015 (H.R. 1314), Congress repealed the automatic enrollment requirement.

Small Group Market Only: All 10 Essential Health Benefits Must Be Covered

The ACA identifies 10 health benefits as essential health benefits. The ten essential health benefits are:

1. Ambulatory patient services
2. Emergency services
3. Hospitalization
4. Maternity and newborn care
5. Mental health, behavior health, and substance abuse services
6. Prescription drug coverage
7. Rehabilitation services and devices
8. Laboratory services
9. Preventative and wellness care, including chronic disease management
10. Pediatric care, including dental and vision care for children until they reach age 19.[35]

---

33. *See* 42 U.S.C. § 300gg-19(a).
34. *See* below, page 17.
35. *See* 45 C.F.R. § 156.110(a).

Insured plans in the small employer market must provide coverage that is substantially equal to the coverage of these benefits by the designated "benchmark" plan for that state.[36] Although it may seem counterintuitive, neither large employer plans nor self-insured plans are required to provide all ten essential benefits or to coordinate with a benchmark plan.[37]

Essential health benefits cannot be subject to lifetime or annual limits. Even though a large employer plan or a self-insured plan is not required to offer all ten essential benefits, if it does it cannot subject that benefit to a lifetime or annual limit.[38]

Exceptions to the Rules for Grandfathered Health Plans

Employer-sponsored group health plans that were in effect on March 23, 2010, and have provided continuous coverage ever since are considered "grandfathered" plans. A grandfathered plan enjoys exemption from several of the ACA's requirements as long as it retains its grandfathered status. Nevertheless, grandfathered plans must comply with most of the same ACA requirements as non-grandfathered plans. A plan that wishes to maintain grandfathered status may continue to enroll new employees and add the

---

36. *See* 42 U.S.C. § 300gg–6(a); 42 U.S.C. § 300gg–11(a)(1); 45 C.F.R. §§ 156.100, 156.110, and 156.115. The benchmark plan for 2016 is one sold in 2012. For 2017, the benchmark plan will be one sold in 2014. The federal Department of Health and Human Services will reconsider the use and structure of benchmark plans after 2017. *See* U.S. Department of Health and Human Services, Centers for Medicare and Medicaid Services, Center for Consumer Information and Insurance Oversight, *Information on Essential Health Benefits (EHB) Benchmark Plans*, www.cms.gov/cciio/resources/data-resources/ehb.html.

37. To use North Carolina as an example, the benchmark plan for years 2017 and following is Blue Cross Blue Shield of North Carolina Blue Options PPO with the required benchmark supplemental pediatric vision and dental plans MetLife Federal Dental Plan–High Option and BCBS Association FEP Blue Vision–High Option. To find the benchmark plan for small employers for years 2017 and following for any state, *see* U.S. Department of Health and Human Services, Centers for Medicare and Medicaid Services, https://www.cms.gov/CCIIO/Resources/Data-Resources/Downloads/Final-List-of-BMPs_2.pdf and *Essential Health Benefits: List of the Largest Three Small Group Products by State—Revised*, https://www.cms.gov/CCIIO/Resources/Regulations-and-Guidance/Downloads/Top3ListFinal-5-19-2015.pdf.

38. *See* 42 U.S.C. § 300gg–11(a)(1); 29 C.F.R. §§ 2590.715-2711(a), (b), and (c).

family members of current and new employees. It may amend the plan to comply with federal and state requirements. It may even increase the cost of the plan's premiums and still keep its grandfathered status.[39] The U.S. Department of Labor has said that it expects all employer-sponsored health plans to have transitioned out of grandfathered status and to be covered by the ACA in full by the end of the decade, but there is in fact no expiration date for grandfathered plans. As long as a plan continues to meet the requirements for keeping grandfathered status, it will remain subject to a less exacting set of requirements. For plans that offer a choice of benefits packages (for example, an 80/20 preferred provider organization plan or a 70/30 plan with a more limited circle of providers), each benefit package must independently qualify for grandfathered status.

ACA Rules That Apply to Grandfathered Plans

Grandfathered plans are subject to most but not all of the new rules that affect other employer-sponsored health insurance plans.

Dependent Coverage Required

As discussed on page 10 above, the ACA requires that group health plans offer coverage for employees' children up to age 26. This requirement applies equally to grandfathered plans.[40]

Enrollment Waiting Period Limited to 90 Days

As discussed on page 9 above, the ACA provides that employees eligible for an offer of coverage must receive that offer within 90 days of beginning employment. This provision applies equally to grandfathered plans.[41]

---

39. *See* 29 C.F.R. §§ 2590.715-1251 (a)–(d).

40. *See* 26 C.F.R. §§ 54.9815-1251T(d) and (e)(2); 29 C.F.R. §§ 2590.715-1251(d) and (e)(2); 45 C.F.R. §§ 147.140(d) and (e)(2).

41. *See* 26 C.F.R. § 54.9815-1251T(d); 29 C.F.R. § 2590.715-1251(d); 45 C.F.R. § 147.140(d).

Pre-existing Condition Exclusions Not Permitted

As discussed on page 9 above, the ACA requires that group health plans must eliminate exclusions for pre-existing conditions entirely. This provision applies equally to grandfathered plans.[42]

No Lifetime or Annual Limits on Essential Health Benefits

As discussed on page 8 above, the ACA prohibits group health plans from imposing annual caps on essential health benefits. This provision applies equally to grandfathered plans.[43]

No Rescission of Coverage

As discussed above on page 11, the ACA prohibits group health plans from rescinding health insurance coverage except in the case of fraud or where the employee has intentionally withheld or mischaracterized information provided to the employer or insurer. This provision applies equally to grandfathered plans.[44]

Summary of Benefits and Coverage

Grandfathered plans, like other health plans, must provide to covered employees a summary of benefits and coverage that includes uniform definitions of standard insurance terms and medical terms; a description of the coverage provided by the plans, including cost-sharing for each of the categories of the ten essential health benefits and for other benefits; exceptions, reductions, and limitations on coverage; cost-sharing provisions, including deductible, co-insurance, and co-payment obligations; information on the renewability and continuation of coverage provisions; and a coverage facts label that includes examples to illustrate common benefits scenarios, including pregnancy and serious or chronic medical conditions and related cost-sharing, such scenarios to be based on recognized clinical practice guidelines. The summary must also include a statement of whether the plan or coverage provides minimum essential coverage and ensures that the plan

---

42. *See* 26 C.F.R. § 54.9815-1251T(e)(1); 29 C.F.R. § 2590.715-1251(e)(1); 45 C.F.R. § 147.140(e)(1).

43. *See* 26 C.F.R. §§ 54.9815-1251T(d) and (e)(1); 29 C.F.R. §§ 2590.715-1251(d) and (e)(1); 45 C.F.R. §§ 147.140(d) and (e)(1).

44. *See* 26 C.F.R. § 54.9815-1251T(d); 29 C.F.R. § 2590.715-1251(d); 45 C.F.R. § 147.140(d).

or coverage share of the total allowed costs of benefits provided under the plan or coverage is not less than 60% of such costs.[45]

Rules That Do Not Apply to Grandfathered Plans

The value of being a grandfathered plan is that the plan sponsor—that is, employers subject to the employer mandate—may offer plans that do not meet some of the ACA requirements. ACA requirements that do not apply to grandfathered plans are as follows.

Mandatory Coverage of Preventative Care and Immunizations with No Cost-Sharing

As discussed above on page 7, the ACA requires group health plans to cover specified preventative care services and immunizations at no cost to the employee or employee's beneficiary. Grandfathered plans are not subject to this requirement.[46]

Limits on Employee Cost-Sharing

As discussed on page 8 above, the ACA imposes limits on the amounts of co-pays, co-insurance, deductibles, and other cost-sharing payments an employee may be required to make. In general, those limits are $7,150 for an individual for a year and $14,300 for a family for a year in 2017, subject to adjustment for inflation. The limits are updated annually by the U.S. Department of Health and Human Services and the IRS. As long as a grandfathered plan retains its grandfathered status, it is not bound by this limitation and may impose co-pays, deductibles, and other employee payments in excess of these amounts without limit.[47]

---

45. *See* 42 U.S.C. § 300gg-15; 26 C.F.R. § 54.9815-1251T(d); 29 C.F.R. § 2590.715-1251(d); 45 C.F.R. § 147.140(d). *See* also U.S. Department of Labor, *FAQs about Affordable Care Act Implementation (Part 30)*, (March 11, 2016), www.dol.gov/EBSA/faqs/faq-aca30.html.

46. *See FAQs about Affordable Care Act Implementation (Part XXVI)* and *FAQs about Affordable Care Act Implementation (Part XXIX) and Mental Health Parity Implementation* (October 23, 2015), www.dol.gov/EBSA/faqs/faq-aca29.html.

47. *See FAQs about Affordable Care Act Implementation (Part XXVII)*.

OB-GYN Choice

The ACA requires health plans to permit female employees to select the obstetrics and gynecological professionals of their choice. Grandfathered plans do not have to meet this requirement, as long as they retain their grandfathered status.

Rules Governing the Claims Review Process

As discussed on page 12 above, the ACA requires group health plans to provide certain appeals rights and allow employees to continue to receive coverage during the appeals process. As long as a grandfathered plan retains its grandfathered status, it is not bound by the ACA's claims requirements.[48]

Maintaining Grandfathered Status

In addition to maintaining the group health plan in substantially the same form as it existed on March 23, 2010, there are several formal steps an employer must take to keep a plan's grandfathered status. First, it must include a statement in any materials about plan benefits that the plan believes itself to be a grandfathered health plan within the meaning of Section 1251 of the ACA, and it must provide contact information for questions or complaints.[49] Second, a plan must maintain records that document the terms of the plan as they existed on March 23, 2010, and any other

---

48. There is one final rule from which grandfathered plans are exempt, but it is not likely to be of interest to local government employers. The IRS has long required that employer self-funded group health plans may not discriminate in favor of higher compensated individuals. That is, top executives could not receive health care benefits that were better than those received by other employees. This rule did not apply to employer health coverage that was not self-funded; that is, where an employer purchased insurance for its employee health coverage, it could discriminate in coverage in favor of highly compensated employees. The ACA extends the non-discrimination provision to such non-self-funded employer health coverage. So, now, all employer-provided health plans must not discriminate in favor of highly compensated individuals, except for grandfathered health plans. If an employer had a non-self-funded plan that did in fact discriminate and the plan qualifies as a grandfathered plan, the employer may continue to use the discriminatory provisions as long as the plan retains its grandfathered status.

49. The U.S. Department of Labor has drafted the model language for adaptation by employers in satisfying this requirement. It can be found at 26 C.F.R. § 54.9815-1251T(a)(2)(ii); 29 C.F.R. § 2590.715-1251(a)(2)(ii); 45 C.F.R. § 147.140(a)(2)(ii). *See also* U.S. Department of Labor, www.dol.gov/ebsa/grandfatherregmodelnotice.doc.

documents necessary to prove its claim that it has a right to grandfathered status.[50] These records must be available for inspection by any federal or state agency and any employee or family member participant for as long as the plan claims grandfathered status.[51]

Losing Grandfathered Status

The ACA itself does not address the point at which changes to a group health plan are sufficient for the plan to lose its grandfathered status. That detail was left to the Departments of Labor, Health and Human Services, and the Treasury to work out in the implementing regulations. The interim final rules on grandfathered status provide that in general, changes to a health plan's benefit package—such as eliminating coverage of a condition or a treatment, increasing co-pays and co-insurance, or decreasing the amount an employer contributes to the cost of premiums—will cause a plan to lose grandfathered status and the exemptions grandfathered status provides. A plan loses its grandfathered status if one of the following six things happens.

Benefits for a Particular Condition Are Eliminated

A plan loses its grandfathered status if all (or substantially all) benefits to diagnose or treat a particular condition are eliminated. If a plan formerly provided benefits for mental health counseling but later eliminated those benefits, it would lose its grandfathered status.[52]

---

50. *See* 26 C.F.R. § 54.9815-1251T(a)(3)(i); 29 C.F.R. § 2590.715-1251(a)(3)(i); 45 C.F.R. § 147.140(a)(3)(i). The preamble to the Interim Final Regulations explains that the following kinds of documents might be needed: intervening and current plan documents, health insurance policies, certificates or contracts of insurance, summary plan descriptions, documentation of premium costs or the cost of coverage, and documentation of required employee contribution rates. *See* 75 Fed. Reg. 34538, 34541 (June 17, 2010).

51. *See* 26 C.F.R. § 54.9815-1251T(a)(3)(ii); 29 C.F.R. § 2590.715-1251(a)(3)(ii); 45 C.F.R. § 147.140(a)(3)(ii).

52. *See* 26 C.F.R. § 54.9815-1251T(g)(1)(i); 29 C.F.R. § 2590.715-1251(g)(1)(i); 45 C.F.R. § 147.140(g)(1)(i).

Co-insurance Percentage Increases

Any increase in the percentage upon which a co-insurance payment is based triggers the loss of grandfathered status.[53] If a plan formerly required that employees pay a 15% co-insurance payment for certain kinds of procedures, then later increased that percentage to 20%, it would lose its grandfathered status. This restriction is based on the fact that as medical costs rise, the dollar amount an employee pays as a percentage of cost will also rise. If in year one, a surgeon charged $5,000 for a procedure, for example, and an employee's co-insurance cost was 20%, the plan would be responsible for $4,000 of the surgery's cost and the employee would be responsible for $1,000. If in year two the surgeon continued to charge $5,000 for the procedure, but the employer group health plan increased the employee's co-insurance to 25%, the employer would be responsible for $3,750 of the surgery's cost and the employee would pay $1,250. The increase in the co-insurance percentage would amount to a significant decrease in benefits under the plan for the employee. If, as is all too common, the surgeon's fee increased in year two but the employee's co-insurance remained at 20%, the dollar amount the employee would pay would be greater, but not because of any change to the plan. Employer and employee would share the increase in the surgeon's fee proportionately. If the surgeon's fee increased and the employee's co-insurance percentage increased, the employee's costs would increase significantly and the employee would bear a disproportionate amount of the increase in cost. For this reason, the regulations relating to grandfathered status do not permit any increase in employees' co-insurance percentage, but do allow limited increases in employee fixed-amount cost-sharing, such as co-pays or deductibles.[54] An employer remains free to increase the co-insurance percentage for which employees are responsible under its group health plan, but the plan will lose its grandfathered status and will then have to comply with all of the ACA's regulations governing health plans.

---

53. *See* 26 C.F.R. § 54.9815-1251T(g)(1)(ii); 29 C.F.R. § 2590.715-1251(g)(1)(ii); 45 C.F.R. § 147.140(g)(1)(ii).

54. *See* the preamble to the Interim Final Regulations at 75 Fed. Reg. 34543.

Cost-Sharing Increases Other than Co-payment Increases above a Certain Percentage

If a fixed-amount payment requirement other than a co-payment, such as a deductible or an out-of-pocket limit, is increased by more than the rate of medical inflation from March 23, 2010, plus 15 percentage points, grandfathered status is lost.[55] The government determines the medical inflation rate.[56]

Fixed-Amount Co-payment Increases above a Certain Amount

If a co-payment amount is increased by more than the rate of medical inflation plus 15 percentage points, or by more than 5 times the rate of medical inflation, grandfathered status is lost.[57] In the case of fixed amount cost-sharing, whether for co-payments or deductibles and out-of-pocket limits, these narrowly circumscribed limited increases are permitted to allow employer plans to keep up with rising medical costs.

Employer Contribution Decreases beyond a Certain Level

If an employer's percentage contribution toward the total cost of coverage for any tier of coverage for any class of similarly situated individuals decreases by more than 5% below its contribution rate on March 23, 2010, grandfathered status is lost.[58]

Imposition of or Decrease in Overall Annual Limits

If previously neither a lifetime nor an annual limit existed and an annual limit is imposed, grandfathered status is lost. If previously there was a lifetime limit but no annual limit, grandfathered status is lost if an annual limit

---

55. *See* 26 C.F.R. § 54.9815-1251T(g)(1)(iii); 29 C.F.R. § 2590.715-1251(g)(1)(iii); 45 C.F.R. § 147.140(g)(1)(iii).

56. The medical inflation rate is determined by reference to the overall medical care component of the Consumer Price Index for All Urban Consumers, unadjusted (CPI), as published by the U.S. Department of Labor. *See* the preamble to the Interim Final Regulations at 75 Fed. Reg. 34543.

57. *See* 26 C.F.R. § 54.9815-1251T(g)(1)(iii); 29 CFR § 2590.715-1251(g)(1)(iii); 45 CFR § 147.140(g)(1)(iii).

58. *See* 26 C.F.R. § 54.9815-1251T(g)(1)(v); 29 C.F.R. § 2590.715-1251(g)(1)(v); 45 C.F.R. § 147.140(g)(1)(v).

less than the lifetime limit is imposed. If previously there was an annual limit and that limit is decreased, grandfathered status is lost.[59]

These are the only changes to an employer-sponsored group health plan that will result in the loss of grandfathered status. Increases in the cost of premiums, decisions by the employer to comply with ACA provisions to which a grandfathered plan does not have to adhere, changes in networks of participating providers, or changes from insured to self-insured status, to take a few examples, will not result in the loss of grandfathered status.[60]

To maintain the grandfathered status of their health insurance plans, employers must provide annual notice to the plan's participants and ensure that they maintain records documenting the plan's terms as of March 23, 2010, the day the ACA was enacted.

Premium Increases

Both grandfathered and non-grandfathered plans may increase the cost of their premiums. But if the increase in the cost of the premium results in the plan no longer being affordable and a single employee receives a premium tax credit, the employer will be liable for the inadequate-coverage penalty.

The ACA's Requirements of Affordability and Minimum Value

An employer of 50 or more full-time employees must offer health insurance coverage that is "affordable" and provides "minimum value" to full-time employees and dependents or face penalties. If the employer fails to (or chooses not to) offer coverage to at least 95% of its full-time employees, it is open to a no-coverage penalty—sometimes called the Section 4980H(a) penalty after the applicable section of the Internal Revenue Code. But even if the employer does offer coverage to 95% of its employees, a second possible penalty kicks in if the coverage offered either is not affordable or does not provide minimum value.

---

59. *See* 26 C.F.R. § 54.9815-1251T(g)(1)(vi); 29 C.F.R. § 2590.715-1251(g)(1)(vi); 45 C.F.R. § 147.140(g)(1)(vi).

60. *See* the preamble to the Interim Final Regulations at 75 Fed. Reg. 34544.

This second kind of penalty is the inadequate-coverage penalty—sometimes called the Section 4980H(b) penalty. This inadequate-coverage penalty kicks in only if at least one employee receives a premium tax credit to help pay for coverage purchased on the exchanges set up under the ACA.

Defining "Affordable" Health Care Coverage

Affordability is assessed in relation to the cost of employee-only insurance coverage.[61] For health insurance coverage to be affordable with respect to any particular employee, the employee's contribution toward the premium for employee-only coverage must not exceed 9.5% of the employee's household income for the year.[62] Although the required contribution percentage of 9.5% is set forth in the text of the ACA, the statute requires the U.S. Department of Health and Human Services to update the percentage every year by the ratio of premium growth in the preceding calendar year to income growth in that year.[63] For 2016, the required contribution percentage was 9.66%.[64] For 2017, the required contribution percentage is 9.69%.[65]

Safe Harbors

How is an employer to know whether the required contribution for an employee exceeds 9.66% (or the applicable updated percentage) of the employee's household income? An employer is, almost surely, not going to know what the employee's household income is. Given that reality, the regulations provide three options for employers to use to check that each

---

61. *See* 26 C.F.R. § 136B-2(c)(3)(v)(A)(2).

62. *See* 26 U.S.C. § 36B(c)(2)(C)(1).

63. *See* 26 U.S.C. § 36B(c)(2)(C)(iv). *See also* Internal Revenue Service, *Rev. Proc. 2014-37*, at https://www.irs.gov/pub/irs-drop/rp-14-37.pdf and Notice 2015-87, *Further Guidance on the Application of the Group Health Plan Market Reform Provisions of the Affordable Care Act to Employer-Provided Health Coverage and on Certain Other Affordable Care Act Provisions* (hereinafter *Further Guidance on the Application of the Group Health Plan Market Reform Provisions,* at https://www.irs.gov/pub/irs-drop/n-15-87.pdf. In Notice 2015-87, the IRS says it plans to amend the employer-mandate regulations to clarify that the 9.5% required contribution percentage is to be updated annually.

64. *See* Internal Revenue Service, *Rev. Proc. 2014-62,* https://www.irs.gov/pub/irs-drop/rp-14-62.pdf and *Further Guidance on the Application of the Group Health Plan Market Reform Provisions.*

65. *See* Internal Revenue Service, *Rev. Proc. 2016-26,* https://www.irs.gov/pub/irs-drop/rp-16-24.pdf.

employee's required contribution is affordable within the meaning of the ACA. Each of these options is termed a "safe harbor." That is, if an employer can determine that an employee's required contribution is affordable using one of these options, then the employer will not be subject to the inadequate-coverage penalty—even if there exists one or more employees for whom the required contribution actually exceeds the adjusted required contribution percentage (9.66% in 2016, 9.69% in 2017) of the employee's actual household income.

Use of the safe harbors is optional. Employers may use different safe harbors for different categories of employees so long as its categories are reasonable and the safe harbor is applied consistently to all members of a category. Reasonable categories include "specific job categories, nature of compensation (for example, salaried or hourly), geographic location, and similar bona fide business criteria." A category unreasonable on its face would be one that simply lists certain employees by name.[66]

Option #1: The Form W-2 wages safe harbor. If the amount of an employee's required yearly contribution to employee-only coverage is less than the adjusted required contribution percentage (9.66% in 2016, 9.69% in 2017) of the amount reported for the calendar year on the employee's IRS Form W-2, the affordability requirement is met. This determination is made after the end of the calendar year when the Form W-2 is prepared. To use the Form W-2 safe harbor, the employee's required contribution must be the same amount throughout the calendar year.[67] For variable-hour employees or new employees who join in the middle of a calendar year, the Form W-2 safe harbor may be used if the employer

- adjusts the Form W-2 wages to reflect only that part of the year during which health coverage was offered,
- adds together the amount of the employee's required contributions for the period for which coverage was offered, and
- determines that the total amount of the employee's required contributions does not exceed 9.66% (or the applicable update percentage) of the adjusted amount of Form W-2 wages.

---

66. *See* 26 C.F.R. § 54-4980H-5(e)(2)(i).
67. *See* 26 C.F.R. § 54-4980H-5(e)(2)(ii)(A).

An employee who is offered coverage for or who works only one day in a calendar month is counted as having worked the entire month for the purpose of the Form W-2 safe harbor.[68]

Option 2: The rate of pay safe harbor. This safe harbor is calculated on a monthly basis. For employees paid on an hourly basis, the employer takes an employee's hourly rate of pay and multiplies it by 130, which is the number of hours treated as a full working month. If the employee's contribution to health coverage is less than 9.66% (or the applicable updated percentage) of that total, then the coverage is "affordable." For salaried employees, the question is whether the employee's contribution is less than 9.66% (or the applicable updated percentage) of that month's salary. Employers who use a weekly or bi-monthly payroll may convert the payroll periods to monthly salary. However, if a salaried employee's salary is reduced in any month for any reason (some examples might include full-day disciplinary suspensions without pay, unpaid FMLA leave, or leave taken in the absence of accrued paid leave), the rate of pay safe harbor may *not* be used. As with the Form W-2 safe harbor, if coverage is offered for at least one day during a calendar month, the entire calendar month is counted for determining the employee's income and his or her premium contribution.[69]

Option 3: The federal poverty line safe harbor. This safe harbor is designed to allow an employer to know with certainty that the contribution required of any employee is "affordable." Like the rate of pay safe harbor, this determination of affordability is made on a monthly basis. An employer takes the published federal poverty line for its state for a single individual for the applicable year and divides it by 12 to get a monthly figure. If an employee's required contribution for that month is less than 9.66% (or the applicable updated percentage) of that figure, it is affordable. If coverage is offered for at least one day during a calendar month, the entire calendar month is counted for determining the employee's income and his or her premium contribution.[70]

Must an employer select only one of the safe harbors or can it use a combination? In the preamble to the employer mandate regulations, the IRS says:

These safe harbors are all optional. An employer may choose to use one or more of these safe harbors for all of its employees or for any

---

68. *See* 26 C.F.R. § 54-4980H-5(e)(2)(ii)(B).
69. *See* 26 C.F.R. § 54-4980H-5(e)(2)(iii).
70. *See* 26 C.F.R. § 54-4980H-5(e)(2)(iv).

reasonable category of employees, provided it does so on a uniform and consistent basis for all employees in a category. . . [R]easonable categories include specific job categories, nature of compensation (for example, salaried or hourly), geographic location, and similar bona fide business criteria.[71]

Employers may not, therefore, use different safe harbors for different individuals. They may, however, use different safe harbors for different groups of employees, so long as those groupings are reasonable and not arbitrary.

Wellness Program Incentives

Some employer wellness programs offer employees discounts on the cost of health insurance premium contributions if an employee meets certain participation or health-outcome requirements. Wellness incentives or rewards related to tobacco use must be treated as earned for all employees, whether or not they have actually satisfied the requirement. In other words, in calculating the affordability or minimum value of a plan, an employer must use the premium or cost-sharing contribution charged to employees who do not use tobacco and to employees who attend or complete tobacco cessation programs, regardless of whether or not an employee is currently using tobacco products. Incentives unrelated to tobacco use, in contrast, are to be treated as unearned by any employee for the purposes of calculating affordability and minimum value. These rules apply to both participatory (rewards based solely upon participation, not on the participant's achievement of a health-related goal) and health-contingent (rewards depending on an employee meeting a health-related goal) wellness programs.[72]

Let's apply this rule to the following hypothetical situations.

> *The City of Paradise offers a wellness program that eliminates monthly premiums for employees who do not use tobacco products or who complete a smoking cessation course (whether or not they actually stop smoking). Jody does not use tobacco and contributes nothing toward the cost of her monthly premiums; the city pays the entire monthly premium. Jordan, on the other hand, is a smoker. He must*

---

71. *See Preamble to Shared Responsibility for Employers Regarding Health Coverage, Final Rule,* 79 Fed. Reg. 8544, 8564 (February 12, 2014).

72. *See* 26 C.F.R. §§ 1.36B-6(2) and 1-36B-2(4).

make a $100 per month or $1,200 annual contribution toward the cost of his premium.

For the purpose of determining the affordability of the city's health coverage, both Jody and Jordan are treated as having earned the tobacco-reduction incentive. In other words, both are treated as having to make no out-of-pocket contributions to the cost of their health insurance premiums. This is clearly an advantage to employers in determining affordability.

Paradise County offers a different sort of incentive to its employees. The county will waive employees' contributions to the cost of their health insurance premiums if they complete cholesterol screenings within the first six months of the plan year. Peter has a cholesterol screening in September, the third month of the plan year, and is refunded the cost of his contributions for July through September and makes no monthly contributions toward the cost of his premium for the remainder of the year. Pam doesn't bother with the cholesterol screening. As a result, she pays $150 per month or $1,800 per year toward the cost of her health insurance premiums.

To determine the affordability of the county's health coverage, both Peter and Pam are treated as *not* having earned the cholesterol screening discount. In other words, both are treated as having to contribute $150 per month toward the cost of health insurance premiums. This is so even though in reality Peter pays nothing. This is not to an employer's advantage in determining affordability.

Health Reimbursement Accounts (HRAs)

Employers who offer health reimbursement accounts (discussed in greater detail on pages 71–74 below) should note that any amounts in an HRA available to an employee for use in paying the employee's share of the employee-only premium, to pay for cost-sharing amounts such as co-pays or deductibles, or to pay for health benefits not covered by the employer's plan count towards the employee's required contribution.[73] This is only fair since HRAs are funded only by employer contributions.

---

73. The employer contribution to the HRA, however, must be required under the terms of the HRA or must be determined before the date on which employees must decide on whether to enroll in the employer's health plan.

The IRS gives the following example of how this works.

FACTS: The employee contribution for health coverage under the major medical group health plan offered by the employer is generally $200 per month. For the current plan year, the employer makes newly available $1,200 under an HRA that the employee may use to pay the employee share of contributions for the major medical coverage, pay cost-sharing, or pay towards the cost of vision or dental coverage. The HRA satisfies all requirements for integration with the major medical group health plan as provided in Notice 2013-54.

CONCLUSION: The $1,200 employer contribution to the HRA reduces the employee's required contribution for the coverage . . . . [because] the employee's required contribution for the major medical plan is $100 ($200 – $100) per month . . . 1/12th of the $1,200 HRA amount per month is [considered] an *employer* contribution whether or not the employee uses the HRA to pay the employee share of contributions for the major medical coverage.[74]

The use of a health reimbursement arrangement does not affect the availability of the affordability safe harbors outlined above. The safe harbors allow an employer to assume what an individual employee's total household income is for the purpose of assessing the affordability of his or her required premium contribution. The employer's contribution to an HRA has the effect of lowering the employee's required contribution and making it, therefore, more likely to be affordable and less likely to result in an employer-mandate penalty.

Employer Contributions to Flexible Spending Accounts (FSAs)
Health care flexible spending accounts are employer-maintained accounts for use in paying unreimbursed medical expenses. Most FSAs are funded only by employees who make contributions on a pre-tax basis through salary reduction. But employers may also make contributions to FSAs.

If employees are not allowed to choose to receive the amount of an employer contribution to an FSA in cash as a taxable benefit, and if the employer contribution may be used to pay for minimum essential coverage

---

74. *See Further Guidance on the Application of the Group Health Plan Market Reform Provisions.*

(see below) and may only be used to pay for medical care, then the amount of the employer contribution may be used to reduce the amount of the employee contribution to the cost of self-only coverage for purposes of determining whether the employer's health plan is affordable.[75]

As in the example above, if an employee's share of the employer-sponsored health insurance premium is $200 per month and the employer contributes $1,200 per year or $100 per month to an employee's FSA (and the contribution cannot be exchanged for cash and may be used to pay the employee's share of the premium and may only be used for medical expenses), then the employee's contribution to the cost of self-only coverage is $100 ($200 – $100).

If the employer allowed the employee to take the $100 per month as a taxable bonus instead of keeping it in the FSA on a pre-tax basis, the $100 per month contribution could not be subtracted from the employee's contribution to the cost of health care coverage, which would remain at $200 per month. If the employer allowed the $100 per month to be used for either medical expenses or dependent care expenses at the employee's discretion, then again the $100 per month contribution could not be subtracted from the employee's contribution to the cost of health care coverage, which would remain at $200 per month. It is clearly to the employer's benefit to limit use of its own contributions to an FSA to payment of medical expenses, including the payment of the employee's share of a health plan premium, on a pre-tax basis.

The reasoning behind this distinction between the uses to which an employer contribution to an FSA may be put is that where employee use of the employer contribution is limited to payment of medical expenses, presumably employees will put that contribution toward the payment of their share of the health insurance premium and, therefore, for affordability purposes, it is reasonable to reduce the cost of their contribution by the same amount. If employees could take the employer contribution as cash or could use it for dependent care expenses, then such an assumption would not be warranted, as employees might well use it to take a trip or to pay for

---

75. *See Further Guidance on the Application of the Group Health Plan Market Reform Provisions.*

part of a daycare or after-school program for their children. Their cost of contribution would not, in this case, be reduced.[76]

For a discussion of how to report employer contributions to an FSA for ACA reporting purposes, see page 75.

Opt-Out Arrangements

Unconditional opt-out arrangements. Employers sometimes offer a taxable cash payment to employees who decline to enroll in the employer's health insurance plan. Sometimes the offer is made in response to a request from an employee who is enrolled in a spouse's employer plan and thinks that the employer should be spending the same amount on similarly situated employees regardless of whether an employee is enrolled in the employer's health insurance plan. Sometimes employers give employees the opportunity to opt out because they think the opt-out option will reduce their health insurance premium costs. The IRS refers to such offers as "unconditional opt-out arrangements." Whatever an employer's reason for offering this option, unconditional opt-out arrangements will likely increase the amount of the employee's required contribution for affordability purposes and may therefore increase the likelihood that an employer will have to pay an inadequate-coverage penalty.

When an employer offers its employees a cash payment conditioned on an employee declining coverage in the employer's health plan, it puts employees in the position of having to choose between cash compensation or health insurance coverage. In other words, because the cost of choosing insurance coverage is foregoing cash compensation, the cost of the health coverage increases. So if an employer who requires employees to make a monthly contribution of $200 toward the cost of employee-only coverage now offers a cash payment of $1,200 per year to any employee who declines the offer of coverage, the employee's required contribution for affordability purposes becomes $300 per month—$200 for the actual premium payment plus $100 for the cash payment the employee has given up.[77]

Offering an opt-out payment is not, therefore, as beneficial to an employer as it may seem at first blush since it increases the amount of the employee's

---

76. *See Further Guidance on the Application of the Group Health Plan Market Reform Provisions.*

77. *See Further Guidance on the Application of the Group Health Plan Market Reform Provisions.*

required contribution and thus increases the likelihood an employer will be liable for an inadequate-coverage penalty.

As of this book's publication date, the IRS has addressed the treatment of unconditional opt-out arrangements only in Notice 2015-87. It intends, however, to issue regulations on this issue in the future. In the interim, employers who offered unconditional opt-out arrangements before December 16, 2015, do not have to add the amount of the opt-out payment to the employee's required contribution cost. Employers who have adopted unconditional opt-out arrangements after December 16, 2015, must include the amount of the opt-out payment in the employee's required contribution cost.[78]

Conditional opt-out arrangements. Sometimes employers offer employees a cash payment in lieu of enrolling in the employer's health plan but only upon satisfaction of a condition—most commonly, upon providing proof of coverage by another health plan, such as one offered by a spouse's employer. As of the date of publication, the IRS has not issued any guidance about whether an employer should treat such an offer as increasing the employee's contribution cost but has said only that it intends to issue rules addressing this question.[79]

Defining *Minimum Value*

For an employer to avoid the inadequate-coverage penalty, its group health plan must be affordable, as described above, and it must provide "minimum value." Minimum value is not defined in the employer-mandate section of the ACA regulations. It is defined in the text of the ACA itself,[80] and is further explained in the ACA regulations as the "percentage of the total allowed

---

78. *See Further Guidance on the Application of the Group Health Plan Market Reform Provisions.* Individual taxpayers may add the amount of an opt-out payment to the cost of contribution for the purposes of qualifying for a premium tax credit, but a premium tax credit allowed on this basis will not result in an employer-mandate penalty in the absence of regulations.

79. *See Further Guidance on the Application of the Group Health Plan Market Reform Provisions.* As with unconditional opt-out arrangements (see preceding note), the IRS has said that individual taxpayers may add the amount of a conditional opt-out payment to the cost of contribution for the purposes of qualifying for a premium tax credit, and that a premium tax credit allowed on this basis will not result in an employer-mandate penalty in the absence of regulations.

80. *See* 26 U.S.C. § 36B(c)(2)(C)(ii).

costs of benefits."[81] An allowed cost is one which an insurer will pay. In other words, a plan provides minimum value if it is designed to pay at least 60% of the total cost of medical services for a standard population.[82]

Minimum value is a complex concept and is a calculation that may be beyond the capacity of an individual employer to make. Nevertheless, here is how minimum value is assessed.

1. The plan must cover at least 60% of the medical costs that could be expected to be incurred under the plan if it applied to a statistically standard population.[83]

2. The benefits offered under the plan must include "substantial coverage" of inpatient hospital services and physician services.[84]

The ACA regulations do not specify what constitutes substantial coverage for this purpose. The preamble to the most recent amendment of this rule, however, explains that the substantial coverage requirement applies to all employer-sponsored health plans, including both those that must provide all 10 essential health benefits and those that do not (i.e., large employer plans, self-insured plans, and grandfathered plans). Even given the requirement of substantial coverage, large employers and self-insured plans still do not have to offer all 10 identified essential health benefits, but the preamble warns that plans that omit inpatient hospital services and physician services "fail to meet universally accepted minimum standards of value expected from, and inherent in the nature of, any arrangement that can reasonably be called a health plan intended to provide the primary health coverage for employees."[85]

---

81. *See* 45 C.F.R. §§ 156.20 and 156.145.

82. *See* the Centers for Medicare & Medicaid Service Center for Consumer Information and Insurance Oversight page on Employer Initiatives at https://www.cms.gov/CCIIO/Programs-and-Initiatives/Employer-Initiatives/Employer-Initiatives.html.

83. *See* 26 U.S.C. § 36B(c)(2)(C)(ii); 45 C.F.R. § 156.20; 45 C.F.R. § 156.145(a).

84. *See* 45 C.F.R. § 156.145(a).

85. *See Preamble to Patient Protection and Affordable Care Act; HHS Notice of Benefit and Payment Parameters for 2016, Final Rule*, 80 Fed. Reg. 10749, 10828 (February 27, 2015). Apparently, under the original version of 45 C.F.R. § 156.145(a), some health plan issuers and employers were representing that plans that offered no coverage of inpatient hospital services or physician services provided minimum value because they satisfied the minimum value 60% rule. *See* 80 Fed. Reg. at 10827.

As a practical matter, employers may have to rely on insurance brokers and issuers to ensure that their plans do in fact provide minimum value, but employers themselves will nonetheless have to report to the IRS that their plan provides minimum value and make the same representation to employees. The U.S. Department of Health and Human Services and the Department of the Treasury have provided a minimum value calculator for employers who wish to determine for themselves whether a plan that provides substantial inpatient hospital services and physician services meets the 60% rule needed to satisfy the minimum value requirement. Employers may enter certain information into the calculator, such as deductibles and co-pays, and the calculator will apply the data related to the statistically standard population and determine whether the plan provides minimum value. (To download the minimum value calculator, Google "aca minimum value calculator" and click on the XLS link for the cms.gov website.)[86]

Minimum Value versus Minimum Essential Coverage (MEC)

As noted on page 12, non-grandfathered plans in the small employer market must provide coverage of all 10 essential health benefits. In addition, *all* health plans must offer minimum essential coverage (MEC) in order to satisfy the employer mandate. Minimum essential coverage is defined by what it is not: minimum essential coverage is any health insurance coverage, including employer-sponsored coverage, consisting of more than merely excepted benefits.[87] Excepted benefits, in turn, are those related to health but not considered health insurance benefits, such as workers' compensation insurance or short- or long-term disability insurance. Excepted benefits also include benefits related to health care offered separately from and not considered a necessary part of a health insurance plan, such as dental or vision insurance, or specialty benefits not coordinated with a health plan, such as freestanding cancer insurance. Excepted benefits can also be policies

---

86. In the Notice of Proposed Rule Making published on December 2, 2015, HHS proposed amending the ACA regulations at 42 C.F.R. § 156.135(g) to provide for regular updating of the minimum value calculator. *See* 80 Fed. Reg. 75488, 75585. For a detailed explanation of the methodology behind the proposed minimum value calculator for 2017, *see* the CMS Memorandum dated November 20, 2015, at https://www.cms.gov/CCIIO/Resources/Regulations-and-Guidance/Downloads/Draft-2017-AVC-Methodology-111915.pdf.

87. *See* 26 U.S.C. § 5000A(f)(1).

that are supplemental to traditional health insurance coverage, such as a Medicare or a TriCare supplement. Thus, a plan that covers only preventative services or only prescription drugs would qualify as offering minimum essential coverage, while one that covers only dental or vision services would not.[88]

Plans that cover only preventative services or prescription drugs, however, do not satisfy the minimum value requirement, since they do not cover inpatient hospital and physician services. Given that fact, why make minimum essential coverage a requirement? Minimum essential coverage is a concept whose origin may be found in the individual mandate—the requirement that each individual enroll in and maintain health insurance coverage greater than that provided by an excepted benefit plan for themselves and their dependents or pay a tax.[89] One way to satisfy the individual mandate is to enroll in an employer-sponsored health plan. To satisfy the employer mandate, an employer-sponsored plan will necessarily offer benefits that meet and, indeed, go beyond the requirements of minimum essential coverage.

The Employer Mandate Penalties

The employer mandate can be stated simply: an employer of 50 or more full-time employees must offer health insurance coverage that is affordable and provides minimum value to full-time employees and dependents or face either a no-coverage penalty or an inadequate-coverage penalty. Whether an employer fails to offer coverage or whether it offers inadequate coverage, it is liable for a penalty tax only if at least one employee receives a premium tax credit to help pay for coverage purchased on the exchanges set up under the ACA. Generally speaking, only individual taxpayers with household incomes between 100% and 400% of the federal poverty line (between 133% and 400% of the federal poverty line in states that have accepted Medicaid expansion assistance under the ACA) are eligible for an ACA premium subsidy.

---

88. *See* 78 Fed. Reg. 218, 220 (Jan. 2, 2013).
89. *See* 26 U.S.C. § 5000A.

The No-Coverage or Section 4980H(a) Penalty

Employers who fail to offer any health insurance coverage at all to their employees (and their dependents), or who fail to offer coverage to more than 5% of their full-time employees (and their dependents), will be liable for the Section 4980H(a) or no-coverage penalty if—and only if—a single one of those employees not offered coverage receives a premium tax credit from the IRS to assist in the purchase of Exchange-based health insurance. The text of the ACA provides that for each month an employer does not offer any coverage or fails to offer coverage to more than 5% of its full-time employees, it will be liable for 1/12 of $2,000 (or $166.67) multiplied by the number of full-time employees it has for that month (excluding employees in a limited non-assessment period; see Part II, pages 84–85). The ACA further provides, however, that the $2,000 benchmark penalty is to increase each year by a percentage defined elsewhere in the statute. For calendar year 2016, the adjusted amount is 1/12 of $2,160 times the number of full-time employees for that month.

The number of full-time employees includes those who enroll in the employer's health insurance plan and those who receive coverage under another plan, such as that offered by a spouse's employer. The number of employees a covered employer has for any month may be reduced by 30 for the purpose of calculating the no-coverage penalty. A shorthand way of calculating the penalty on an annual basis is to multiply the total number of full-time employees minus 30 by $2,160 (or more in years after the 2016 tax year). An employer who does not offer any health insurance at all could be subject to a substantial penalty. There is no partial credit or sliding penalty—if an employer covers 93% of its employees, the penalty is the same as if the employer had covered none of its employees. The penalty is assessed separately for each month of the calendar year but is paid in one lump sum in the following calendar year.

Generally, if an employer fails to offer coverage to an eligible employee for even one day of a month, the employee is deemed not to have been offered coverage for the entire month. An exception to this rule occurs when the employee begins work on any day other than the first day of the month or terminates employment on any day other than the last day of the month. Employees beginning or ending employment on days other than the first or last days of the month will not be counted in the total number of employees for that month for the purpose of calculating the no-coverage penalty.

So if an employer should have offered coverage to 225 employees, but in fact offered coverage to only 213, the employer is not subject to the no-coverage penalty for that month because it offered coverage to 95% of its employees. If, on the other hand, the employer should have offered coverage to 225 employees but in fact offered coverage to only 150, then it will be liable for a penalty of $32,500.65 that month. That figure is reached by multiplying 1/12 of $2000 (or $166.67) by 195 employees (225 full-time employees minus 30). The penalty will be the same for every month in which coverage was offered to only 150 of 225 full-time employees.

An employer can be subject to only one kind of penalty. An employer subject to the no-coverage payment will not be subject to the second type of employer-shared-responsibility payment—namely, the 4980H(b) or inadequate-coverage penalty described below.

The Inadequate-Coverage or Section 4980H(b) Penalty

If a covered employer offers health insurance coverage to all or 95% of its full-time employees and their dependents and one or more of those employees has received a premium tax subsidy to help them purchase health insurance on the Exchange because the employer's policy is not affordable or does not provide minimum value (see pages 21–33 above), the employer will be subject to the Section 4980H(b) or inadequate-coverage penalty. For each month an employer has at least one employee receiving a premium tax credit, it will be liable for 1/12 of $3,000 times the number of employees receiving the premium subsidy. The ACA further provides, however, that the $3,000 benchmark penalty is to increase each year by a percentage defined elsewhere in the statute. For calendar year 2016, the adjusted amount is $3,240 times the number of employees receiving the premium subsidy.

The ACA regulations provide that an employer who offers "inadequate coverage" will never pay more in penalties than an employer who offers no coverage whatsoever: the total amount of the inadequate-coverage penalty is capped at the amount the employer would pay if it had not offered health insurance coverage and were subject to the no-coverage penalty.

As with the no-coverage penalty, if an employer fails to offer affordable coverage providing minimal value to an eligible employee for even one day of a month, the employee is deemed not to have been offered such coverage for the entire month. An exception to this rule is when the employee begins work on any day other than the first day of the month or terminates employment on any day other than the last day of the month. Employees beginning or ending employment on days other than the first or last days of the month will be treated as having been offered coverage for that month for the purposes of the inadequate-coverage penalty.

Notification from the IRS that a No-Coverage or an Inadequate-Coverage Penalty Is Due

Employers will receive notification from the IRS when one or more of their employees have received a premium subsidy. After employees have filed their individual tax returns and employers have filed their ACA information returns, the IRS will give notice to employers of their potential liability for the no-coverage penalty (before making the actual demand for payment) and give them an opportunity to respond.

Part 2

Determining Who Is a Covered Employer

The only employers subject to the employer mandate are those who had 50 or more full-time employees or full-time equivalents (FTEs) during the previous calendar year. These employers are referred to as "applicable large employers" or "ALEs" in the Affordable Care Act (ACA) and its regulations. This book will refer to them simply as "covered employers." Very large employers will know without having to do a tally that they have more than 50 full-time employees and are covered. Likewise, very small municipalities or agencies will also know without counting that they have fewer than 50 full-time employees and are not covered. Employers who do not know whether they have 50 full-time employees or full-time equivalents will have to determine precisely how many full-time equivalents they have as that term is used in the ACA.

Accurate Reporting of Number of Employees Required on Form 1094-C

As discussed more fully above on pages 90–96, the Internal Revenue Service (IRS) requires employers to report annually on Form 1095-C whether it has made an offer of coverage to each full-time employee. The individual forms are first given to employees and then the entire set of Forms 1095-C are sent to the IRS with a summary cover sheet, Form 1094-C. Form 1094-C requires employers to provide the total number of full-time equivalent employees (FTEs) and its total number of employees overall. This means that employers large enough to know right off the bat that they are covered employers must nevertheless count the number of FTEs as that term is defined by the ACA. Very small employers who know they have fewer than 50 FTEs do not need to determine the total number of FTEs for ACA purposes because they will never be required to complete Form 1094-C.

Counting ACA Full-Time Employees

For ACA purposes, a full-time employee is one who works 30 or more hours each week.[1] To determine whether an organization is a covered employer, an employer should do the following.

1. Count the number of its actual full-time employees, including any temporary and seasonal workers for each month.
2. Add together the number of hours worked by each part-time employee each month and divide the total by 120. The result is the number of FTEs for that month.[2]
3. Add together the total number of actual full-time employees and the total number of FTEs for each month and divide the final total by 12.[3]

The result will show whether the employer averaged 50 or more FTEs during the previous calendar year. For example, in a month in which an employer has 39 full-time employees and 20 part-time employees who average 17 hours per week, the employer would be treated as having 50 full-time employees. How do we reach that result?

- 17 hours per week × 20 employees × 4 weeks = 1,360 total hours
- 1,360 total hours / 120 (ACA divisor) = 11.33 FTEs
- 39 F/T employees + 11.33 FTEs = 50 employees

---

1. *See* 26 C.F.R. § 54.4980H-1(a)(21).
2. *See* 26 C.F.R. § 54.4980H-2(c)(2).
3. *See* 26 C.F.R. § 54.4980H-2(b)(1).

Temporary Employees

An employer must count temporary employees in determining whether it has 50 FTEs. Temporary employees who work 30 hours per week should be counted as full-time employees the same way permanent employees who work 30 hours a week are counted. Both groups are full-time employees for the purpose of determining whether an employer is an applicable large employer covered by the ACA. Remember that the total number of full-time employees and FTEs for each month are added up and that this figure is divided by the 12 months of the year. This calculation gives appropriate weight to the fact that some employees are not employed for the entire year.

Independent Contractors

True independent contractors do not count when calculating an employer's number of full-time employees—precisely because they are not employees. The most important factors weighing toward employee, rather than independent contractor, status are the following.

- The hiring organization has the right to control when, where, and how the worker will do the job, or the order and sequence in which the worker will perform services.
- The hiring organization sets the worker's hours and schedule.
- The work must be performed personally by the worker (as opposed to the worker subcontracting it out or furnishing his or her own substitute).
- The hiring organization provides the worker with the tools, supplies, and equipment needed to do the job (as opposed to requiring the worker to bring his or her own tools, equipment, and supplies to the job).
- An employee of the hiring organization supervises the worker.
- The work is performed on the hiring organization's premises or at a site controlled or designated by the hiring organization.
- The worker can be fired at the will of the hiring organization.
- The worker is not guaranteed a set amount of money for the services performed, but may make a profit or suffer a loss depending on the project's outcome.[4]

---

4. For more on independent contractors, see my article, *Independent Contractor or Employee? The Legal Distinction and Its Consequences*, PUBLIC EMPLOYMENT

The bottom line is that for the purposes of the ACA, independent contractors are not included when determining whether an employer has 50 or more full-time employees. It is, of course, a huge mistake for both tax and ACA purposes to mischaracterize an employee as an independent contractor. Merely calling a person an independent contractor does not make it so.

"Leased" Employees

The issue of how to treat leased employees is difficult because there are many different kinds of leasing and staffing arrangements. Generally speaking, however, anyone who performs services for a local government but is not on the local government's payroll and instead is compensated by a staffing company does not count in calculating whether an employer has 50 or more employees and is subject to the employer mandate.

In the most common "leasing" arrangement, an employer fills a temporary need by entering into a contract with a staffing agency. The agency provides a qualified worker; the employer pays the agency a fee for the worker's services; the agency pays the worker's wages. The amount that the employer pays the agency and that the agency pays the worker are not coordinated; each is negotiated independently. Sometimes employers enter into this arrangement for lengthy or indefinite periods of time.

Less common in the public sector is the use of a professional employer organization. A professional employer organization is an employee management company. In this arrangement, the employer hires, trains, and supervises the worker, but outsources the responsibility for paying employees and providing them with insurance and other benefits to a separate company to which it pays a fee.

The ACA regulations define *employee* as "an individual who is an employee under the common-law standard" and *employer* as "the person that is the employer of an employee under the common-law standard."[5] The common-law standard is the same set of factors used to determine whether a worker is an independent contractor or an employee. The regulation's definition of "employee" does provide some additional help in determining whether a "leased" employee is to be counted in determining whether an employer has 50 or more employees: it expressly excludes from the mean-

---

Law Bulletin No. 32, May 2005, http://sogpubs.unc.edu/electronicversions/pdfs/pelb32.pdf.

5. *See* 26 C.F.R. §§ 54.4980H-1(a)(15) and (16) respectively.

ing of employee "a leased employee (as defined in section 414(n)(2))" [of the Internal Revenue Code]. Section 414(n)(2) defines *leased employee as follows*:

. . . . the term "leased employee" means any person who is not an employee of the recipient and who provides services to the recipient if—

(A) such services are provided pursuant to an agreement between the recipient and any other person (in this subsection referred to as the "leasing organization"),

(B) such person has performed such services for the recipient (or for the recipient and related persons) on a substantially full-time basis for a period of at least 1 year, and

(C) such services are performed under primary direction or control by the recipient.

Read together, the definition of *employee* in Section 4980H-1(a)(15) and the definition of *leased employee* in Internal Revenue Code section 414(n)(2) say that persons performing services for a local government who are not on the local government's payroll but are on the payroll of a staffing, leasing, or other employee organization do not count in calculating whether an employer has 50 or more employees and is subject to the employer mandate of the ACA. This is true even when the person has performed services for the government employer for periods in excess of a year.[6]

Seasonal Workers

Employers must count seasonal workers when determining whether they are covered by the ACA, but the ACA regulations provide relief to small employers whose use of temporary employees during certain seasons puts them over the 50-employee threshold.

When counting the number of full-time employees it employs each calendar month, an employer must count seasonal workers in those months in which they work. If the employer had a full-time workforce exceeding 50 employees on only 120 or fewer days (or 4 or fewer calendar months) in the preceding year, *and* the employer only had 50 or more full-time employees

---

6. That being said, the government employer that is the recipient of services may still be a joint employer for other purposes, such as liability under Title VII, just not for ACA purposes.

during those 120 or fewer days because it was employing seasonal workers, the employer may subtract the seasonal workers from its monthly totals.[7] The following two examples illustrate this principle.

Example 1. The town of Paradise Beach has 40 full-time, year-round employees and 45 full-time employees who work only during the months of June, July, August, and September. This means that the town has the equivalent of 320 FTE employees for the combined 8-month period January through May and October through December (40 × 8). It has the equivalent of 340 FTE employees for the 4-month period running June through September (85 × 4). In determining whether the town is covered by the ACA, the human resources director will add the total number of employees the town has employed for each month of the year, namely the 320 employees representing the 8-month January through May and October through December stretch to the 340 employees representing the 4-month period June through September. The sum of 320 plus 340 is 660 FTEs. To get the town's average per month, of course, the human resources director will have to divide 660 by the 12 months of the year. The town averages 55 employees per month.

- *40 F/T employees × 8 months = 320 F/T employees for 8 months of the year*
- *85 F/T employees × 4 months = 340 F/T employees for four months of the year*
- *320 + 340 = 660 full-time employees / 12 months = an average of 55 employees*

In reality, Paradise Beach has those 55 full-time employees (and then some) for only 4 months—June, July, August, and September. During the remaining months of the year, it has only 40 full-time employees. The 5 employees in excess of the 50-employee threshold are attributable solely to the presence of seasonal beach employees. Therefore, Paradise Beach will not be treated as a covered employer for that calendar year.

7. *See* 26 C.F.R. §§ 54.4980H-1(a)(39) and 54.4980H-2(b)(2).

Example 2. *The town of Amazing Beach has 40 full-time, year-round employees and 45 full-time employees who work only during the months of June, July, August, and September. Last year, however, Amazing Beach also had 60 full-time equivalent employees during the month of October assisting in cleanup work after a major hurricane.*

To determine whether Amazing Beach is covered by the ACA, the human resources director first adds together the number of full-time employees working each month from January through May and from October through December. The town has 320 FTEs for those 8 months of the year. Now the human resources director adds together the number of full-time employees working each month from June through September. The town has 340 employees for those 4 months of the year. Together, they add up to 660. The town must also account for the temporary employees who worked during the hurricane cleanup in October, not all of whom worked full time. Together they amounted to 60 FTEs. This number is added to 660 to get 720. The number 720 represents the total number of FTEs the town employed over the course of the year. To get the town's average per month, the human resources director divides 720 by the 12 months of the year. The town averages 60 employees per month.

- *40 F/T employees × 8 months = 320 F/T employees for 8 months of the year*
- *85 F/T employees × 4 months = 340 F/T employees for 4 months of the year*
- *60 FTE employees × 1 month = 60 FTE employees for 1 month of the year*
- *320 + 340 + 60 = 720 full-time employees / 12 months = an average of 60 employees*

The town of Amazing Beach, however, cannot use the seasonal worker exemption. The seasonal worker exemption applies only if the sum of an employer's full-time employees (including seasonal employees) exceeds 50 for 4 months (or 120 days) or fewer. Due to the increased number of employees it had in October, Amazing Beach had more than 50 full-time and FTE employees for 5 months.

Volunteers

Generally speaking, volunteers do not count toward a public employer's total number of employees. The ACA regulations define a volunteer as a person who performs services for a government entity whose only compensation is in the form of either (1) a reimbursement or allowance for reasonable expenses incurred in the performance of services by volunteers or (2) reasonable benefits and nominal fees of a type customarily paid by similar entities in connection with the performance of services by volunteers.[8]

Local governments may therefore continue to reward volunteers with some form of recognition for their service in the form of a cash award—for example, by reimbursing them for expenses or by paying them a nominal amount for each public safety call to which they respond or each parks and recreation game at which they coach or officiate. These small rewards are permissible under the ACA and will not turn volunteers into employees when an employer is determining whether it is a covered employer.

Elected Officials

An employer should not include elected officials when determining whether it meets the 50-employee threshold. This is true even though elected officials who receive a stipend in return for their service are considered employees by the IRS for income-tax reporting purposes and must be issued a W-2 each January.

The ACA regulations define an *employee* as "an individual who is an employee under the common-law standard."[9] Elected officials do not meet the common-law test for determining whether a worker is an employee or an independent contractor, notwithstanding their inclusion as employees for tax withholding purposes. Under the common-law standard for determining whether someone is an employee of an organization, the relevant factors are (1) whether the employer has control over how and when the individual's work is done, control being characteristic of employee status; (2) the employer's right to fire the individual; (3) whether the individual is engaged in an independent business, calling, or occupation; (4) whether the individual is doing the work at a fixed price or for a lump sum or upon a quantitative basis, payment on a quantitative basis being characteristic of an

8. *See* 26 C.F.R. § 56.4980H-1(a)(7).
9. *See* 26 C.F.R. § 54.4980H-1(a)(15).

employee; and (5) whether the individual is free to use such assistants as he or she may think proper and has full control over such assistants.[10]

Elected officials have complete control over how and when they do the work, cannot be fired, generally have other employment (or other sources of income, if retired), are paid a lump-sum stipend regardless of the amount of time they spend on the work, and are free to hire assistants to help in the work at their own expense.

But do elected officials count as employees for the purpose of determining whether an employer must offer health insurance or pay a penalty? The regulations do not expressly address this question, but the answer seems to be no. Elected officials are not employees. To the extent that they must be categorized, they are more akin to volunteers. The only exception to this rule is an elected official such as the elected sheriff or register of deeds who works full-time, earns a full-time salary, and is otherwise entitled to employee benefits, such as retirement benefits.

Employees Covered by TriCare

Employees independently covered by TriCare, the U.S. military's health care system, or by a Veterans Administration health care program should not be counted when determining whether an employer has 50 or more full-time employees.

Overtime Hours

Overtime hours are included when calculating how many employees work 30 hours per week for the purpose of determining whether an employer is covered by the employer mandate. Overtime hours are also included when calculating whether an employee is full-time and must be offered health insurance (see below, page 53).

---

10. *See, for example*, Hayes v. Elon College, 224 N.C. 11, 15 (1944). *See also* Hughart v. Dasco Transp., Inc., 167 N.C. App. 685, 694; Emp't Sec. Comm'n v. Huckabee, 120 N.C. App. 217, 219–220 *aff'd*, 343 N.C. 297 (1995).

Reaching the 50-Employee Threshold for the First Time

Consider the following hypothetical.

> *The town of Paradise has had a full-time workforce that has averaged between 42 and 48 full-time employees for the past eight years. Last year, for the first time, the town averaged 53 full-time employees. Paradise has never offered health insurance to its employees, preferring to pay them higher-than-average wages so they could purchase health insurance on their own.*

The town now has until the next April 1 (that is, the April 1 of the next calendar year following the year in which it first averaged 50 or more full-time employees) to offer affordable health insurance to its employees or face one of the ACA's employer penalties for failure to provide health insurance coverage or failure to provide affordable coverage. The ACA regulations essentially give employers a three-month window in which to realize that they are now covered by the ACA's employer mandate and to find affordable coverage.

If the town was already providing affordable health insurance to its full-time employees, it would not be liable for either of the ACA's employer mandate penalties. It would, however, now be subject to the ACA's reporting requirements. These requirements do not apply to employers with fewer than 50 full-time employees.

Small Employers That Offer Health Insurance

Small employers who offer health insurance to their employees may change their minds at any time and discontinue employee health insurance coverage, as long as they remain below the 50-employee threshold.

Offering Part-Time Employees Health Coverage

An employer may always provide greater benefits than the law requires, so it may offer health insurance coverage to employees who work fewer than 30 hours per week. It may offer health insurance coverage on the same terms as it offers coverage to full-time employees or it may offer coverage with a higher premium contribution than it requires of full-time employees. An employer who offers coverage to part-time employees can change its policy and raise the minimum number of hours needed to participate in the health plan to 30 at any time.

Part 3

Determining Who Must Receive an Offer of Health Coverage

The employer mandate of the Affordable Care Act (ACA) is stated most succinctly as follows: Employers with 50 or more full-time employees must offer health insurance coverage to all full-time employees or face penalties. The ACA has one set of rules for employers to use in determining whether they have the requisite 50 employees to bring them within the law's coverage. These rules were the subject of Part 2 of this book. The ACA has a slightly different set of rules for employers to use in determining who those full-time employees are to whom they must make an offer of coverage. As noted in the previous Part, the ACA defines a full-time employee as one "who is employed *an average of at least 30 hours of service per week* with an employer."[1] The ACA regulations allow employers to treat 130 hours of service in a calendar month as the monthly equivalent of at least 30 hours of service per week.[2] Covered employers must therefore determine the full-time status of each employee and offer affordable coverage to each employee

---

1. *See* 26 C.F.R. § 54.4980H-1(a)(21)(i).

2. *See* 26 C.F.R. § 54.4980H-1(a)(21)(ii). This number was reached by multiplying 30 hours of service per week times 52 weeks divided by 12 months. The Departments of the Treasury, Health and Human Services, and Labor decided to include a monthly equivalency so that there would be no difference in treatment between employees whose hours of service generally occurred on weekends and those whose hours occurred on business days when the day that the first day of a month falls on would mandate coverage for the former, but not for the latter. *See Preamble to Shared Responsibility for Employer Regarding Health Coverage, Final Rule*, 79 Fed. Reg. 8544, 8553 (February 12, 2014).

averaging 30 hours of service per week or 130 hours of service per month. For employees whose weekly hours fluctuate above and below 30 hours, employers will have to continually monitor their hours to remain compliant with the law.

Part 3 will explain the complicated set of rules governing which employees must receive offers of coverage and how and when employers must make those offers.

What Counts As an Hour of Service?

The ACA regulations provide that an hour of service is any hour for which an employee is paid for the performance of duties or paid for a period of time during which no duties are performed due to vacation, holiday, illness, incapacity (including disability), layoff, jury duty, military duty, or leave of absence. Hours that an employee spends performing services as a bona fide volunteer (an employee of the finance department, for example, serving as a parks and recreation department basketball referee) do not count as an ACA hour of service.[3]

If an employee is not working but is receiving workers' compensation benefits, the time spent on workers' compensation leave will count as hours of service.

If an employee is not working but is receiving short- or long-term disability payments, the period of time during which the employee is on leave will not count toward hours of service unless the employer has contributed directly or indirectly to the cost of the disability coverage. Periods of time during which an employee is receiving short- or long-term disability payments from a plan paid for solely by the employee on an after-tax basis do not count as hours of service.[4]

Employees Expected to Work 30 Hours per Week

New employees whom an employer reasonably expects to work an average of 30 hours per week or 130 hours per calendar month must be offered affordable health coverage *no later than the first day of the fourth full calendar*

---

3. *See* 26 C.F.R. § 54.4980H-1(a)(24).

4. *See* IRS Notice 2015-87, *Further Guidance on the Application of the Group Health Plan Market Reform Provisions of the Affordable Care Act to Employer-Provided Health Coverage and on Certain Other Affordable Care Act Provisions*, available at https://www.irs.gov/irb/2015-52_IRB/ar11.html.

month of employment.[5] In determining whether an employee is likely to work the required number of hours, employers may consider the following non-exclusive list of factors:

- whether the employee is replacing an employee who was a full-time employee,
- the extent to which the hours of current employees in the same or comparable positions have fluctuated above and below 30 hours of service per week during recent measurement periods,
- whether the job was advertised as requiring 30 or more hours of service per week, and
- whether the new hire was told that the job required 30 or more hours of service per week.[6]

Tracking the Hours of Employees Whose Average Weekly Hours Cannot Be Predicted

Sometimes an employer does not know whether an employee will average 30 hours a week over a particular work period. That's a problem, because if the employee does average 30 hours, the employer must offer health coverage or pay a penalty. So how is the employer to know? The ACA refers to employees whose average weekly hours of work an employer cannot accurately predict as "variable-hour employees." The ACA regulations provide two methods of calculating whether variable-hour employees are averaging 30 hours of service per week: the monthly measurement method and the look-back measurement method.

Under the monthly measurement method, the employer tracks the actual hours an employee works each month. If in any month the employee averages 30 hours or more, then the employer must offer health coverage. If an employee subsequently falls below 30 hours, the employer could, theoretically, discontinue the employee's coverage. But the employer should ensure that the employee will in fact remain below 30 hours in order to avoid the administrative costs of taking that employee on and off the policy and of offering COBRA continuation coverage multiple times.

---

5. *See* 26 C.F.R. §§ 54.4980H-3(c)(2) and (d)(2)(iii).
6. *See* 26 C.F.R. §§ 54.4980H-1(a)(49); 54.4980H-3(d)(2)(iii).

Under the look-back measurement method, the employer tracks the employee's actual hours over a measurement period, as described below, to see whether over that measurement period the employee is averaging 30 hours. The measurement period is followed by a stability period, during the entirety of which an employee is treated as either full-time or part-time, depending on whether the employee averaged 30 hours per week or fewer than 30 during the preceding measurement period. Neither an employee's status during the stability period nor the employee's eligibility for health coverage changes during the stability period, regardless of how many hours they actually work.

Definitions Related to the Look-Back Measurement Method

standard measurement period. A period of between 3 and 12 months used to measure an employee's hours of service under the look-back measurement method.

initial measurement period. The first standard measurement period for a new employee. *See* 26 C.F.R. § 54.4980H-1(a)(46).

stability period. A fixed period, the length of which is determined by the employer, that immediately follows an initial or standard measurement period and any associated administrative period during which an employee's status as full-time or part-time is fixed. *See* 26 C.F.R. § 54.4980H-1(a)(45). This term is used only in connection with the look-back measurement period.

If an employee did in fact average 30 hours in the measurement period, that employee must be offered health coverage that remains effective throughout the stability period. If the employee did not average 30 hours in the measurement period, the employer does not have to offer coverage during the stability period no matter how many hours the employee actually averages during the stability period. A new measurement period runs concurrently with the stability period and the same principles apply during the stability period that follows the new measurement period. The cycle repeats itself indefinitely unless the employer chooses to treat the employee as a full-time employee, offer health coverage, and stop counting hours worked.

Rules for Measuring Hours of Service Applicable to Both the Monthly Measurement Method and the Look-Back Measurement Method

Hourly Employees

Employers must calculate actual hours of service as reflected in payroll records for all employees paid on an hourly basis.[7] Overtime hours are included when calculating whether an employee works an average of 30 hours per week and must be offered health insurance. Overtime hours would also be included in calculating how many employees work 30 hours per week for the purpose of determining whether an employer is covered by the employer mandate.

Salaried Employees

Employers may choose from among the following methods for calculating the hours of service for salaried employees:

- actual hours of service,
- a days-worked equivalency method: the employer credits an employee who has worked at least 1 hour on a given day with 8 hours of service, or
- a weeks-worked equivalency method: the employer credits an employee who has worked at least 1 hour in a given week with 40 hours of service.[8]

Employers may use different methods for calculating the hours of different categories of salaried employees so long as the categories are reasonable and consistent. *Employers may change the method they use for calculating the hours of a given group of salaried employees each calendar year, but not more frequently.*[9]

---

7. *See* 26 C.F.R. § 54.4980H-3(b)(2). Keep in mind that some nonexempt employees are paid on a salaried basis. These employees may be treated as salaried employees for the purposes of the ACA employer mandate, but their status under the Fair Labor Standards Act does not change.

8. *See* 26 C.F.R. § 54.4980H-3(b)(3).

9. *See* 26 C.F.R. § 54.4980H-3(b)(3)(ii).

Public Safety and Other Employees with Fluctuating or Flex-Time Schedules

The employer-mandate regulations do not permit employers to use the days-worked or the weeks-worked equivalency methods where the result would be to substantially undercount an employee's hours of service. For example, employees who worked three 10-hour shifts per week would be credited with only 24 hours of work per week if the employer used the days-worked equivalency (8 hours × 3 days). As a result, those employees would be denied full-time status when they in fact worked 30 hours per week and were entitled to participate in the employer's health insurance plan. The rules do not permit this.[10]

Public safety agencies frequently make use of so-called PRN employees, paid substitutes who fill in on an as-needed basis. Each PRN works a different number of hours each week and each month. Employers of PRNs must keep track of each individual PRN's hours using either the monthly measurement method or the look-back measurement method. If an employer knows that a PRN works an average of 30 hours per week (for example, the PRN always works two shifts a week, even though the PRN is always subbing for different people), then the employer must offer the PRN health insurance coverage. If a PRN occasionally works two 24-hour shifts, but mostly works one or fewer, then under either measurement method, the PRN will not average 30 hours and will not have to be offered health insurance. If an employer does not want to have to offer PRNs health insurance, it may have to limit the number of shifts a PRN may cover in a week—a PRN who fills in for a 24-hour shift firefighter, for example, may have to be limited to one shift a week if the employer does not want to have to cover the PRN under its health insurance plan.

Different Measurement Methods and Different Measurement Periods for Different Groups of Employees

The regulations allow employers to use the monthly measurement period for salaried employees and the look-back measurement period for hourly employees and vice versa. Employers using the look-back measurement period may also use different measurement and stability periods for salaried and hourly employees, including using measurement periods of different

---

10. *See* 26 C.F.R. § 54.4980H-3(b)(3)(iii).

lengths for one group or the other or periods with different starting and ending dates. Employers may change from one measurement method to the other and may change the duration or start date of a measurement period under the look-back method.[11]

Notifying Employees

Employers must make an offer of coverage to employees who work an average of 30 hours a week over the course of a measurement period. There is no penalty for failing to notify employees who do not qualify for an offer of coverage, but the far better practice would be to notify them as well.

The following sections will discuss the monthly measurement period and the look-back measurement period in greater detail. Keep in mind that these methods are used to determine whether variable-hour employees—those whose monthly level of service cannot be determined as of their start dates—must be offered health insurance coverage. When an employer knows an employee will be working 30 or more hours per week, there will be no need to count the employee's hours.

The Monthly Measurement Method

To use the monthly measurement method to determine whether a variable-hour employee qualifies for health insurance coverage, an employer counts the actual hours of service a variable-hour employee works each calendar month. If the employee *averages* 30 hours of service per week in any month, the employer must offer coverage that begins with the first day of the first calendar month following a three-month period beginning with the first full calendar month in which the employee averages 30 hours a week.[12] For example, if an employee begins work on November 15, the employer would begin to count that employee's hours on December 1 and, assuming the employee averages 30 hours of service per week in December, the employer would have to offer that employee health insurance coverage effective the following March 1.

To take another example, consider an employee who begins work on February 15. The employer would begin to count the employee's hours of service

---

11. *See* 26 C.F.R. § 54.4980H-3(b)(3)(C)(ii).
12. *See* 26 C.F.R. §§ 54.4980H-3(c)(1) and (2).

on March 1. This employee works fewer than an average of 30 hours per week during the months of March through September. In October, however, the employee averages 30 hours per week. The employer would then have to offer the employee health insurance coverage on January 1.

The Weeks-Worked Equivalency and the Monthly Measurement Method

Calendar months do not, of course, always begin at the beginning of a calendar week or a workweek. Depending on the payroll system an employer uses, this may make tracking employees' monthly hours difficult. The ACA regulations therefore allow employers to use what the regulations call a "weeks-worked equivalency." To use the weeks-worked equivalency, an employer may begin to measure hours of service on the first day of the week that *includes* the first day of the calendar month. If the employer uses this method, it cannot include the week in which the last day of the calendar month falls unless the week ends with the last day of the month.[13] For example, if December 1 falls on a Wednesday, the employer may start the monthly measurement period on Sunday, November 28. In that year, December 31 would fall on a Friday, so the last week of December would not be included in that monthly measurement period, but would begin the next monthly measurement period. Under the weekly equivalency rule, an employee must be treated as full-time if the employee works a minimum of 120 hours during that monthly measurement period (30 hours per week × 4 weeks).[14]

An employer may also begin to measure hours of service on the first day of the week that *follows* the first day of the calendar month. If it uses this method, it must include the week in which the last day of the calendar months falls.[15] If December 1 falls on a Wednesday, the employer may start the monthly measurement period on Monday, December 6. The week of December 31 (which would be a Friday) would be included in the monthly measurement period. Again, because this is a variant of the weekly equivalency rule, employees must be treated as full-time if they work a minimum of 120 hours during that measurement period.[16]

---

13. *See* 26 C.F.R. § 54.4980H-3(c)(3)(i).
14. *See* 26 C.F.R. § 54.4980H-3(c)(5) (Example 3).
15. *See* 26 C.F.R. § 54.4980H-3(c)(3)(ii).
16. *See* 26 C.F.R. § 54.4980H-3 (c)(5) (Example 3).

If in any month the use of the weeks-worked equivalency results in a monthly measurement period of five weeks, then employees are treated as full-time employees if they work at least 150 hours of service for that monthly measurement period (30 hours per week × 5 weeks).[17]

Employees Rehired after Termination or Leave of Absence

In most cases, an employee who does not have any hours of service for a period of 13 consecutive weeks or more may be treated as a new employee for the purpose of determining hours of service.[18] The rule is different for community college and public school employees, many of whom normally work for periods of less than a year. Community college and public school employees who do not have any hours of service for 26 consecutive weeks or more may be treated as new employees for the purpose of determining hours of service.[19]

An employee who has not had any hours of service for a period of *fewer* than 13 weeks (or 26 weeks, if employed by an educational institution) is considered a "continuing employee." A continuing employee must be offered the resumption of coverage by no later than the first full day of the first full month following the day on which the employee returned to work. Consider the following hypothetical.

> *Frank has been a full-time employee of the City of Paradise for several years. In March and April, Frank takes unpaid administrative leave for nine consecutive weeks. When Frank returns to work, he may not be treated as a new hire and subject to a new monthly measurement period because his leave was for fewer than 13 consecutive weeks. The city may, however, treat him as if he were no longer a full-time employee during March and April—in other words, his employer need not offer him health insurance, although it would have to offer him COBRA continuation coverage. If Frank's "special unpaid leave" were FMLA leave, on the other hand, the city would be obligated to continue his health insurance and to continue contributing to it on the same basis as it would were he working and not on leave.*

---

17. *See* 26 C.F.R. § 54.4980H-3(c)(5) (Example 3).
18. *See* 26 C.F.R. § 54.4980H-3(c)(4)(i).
19. *See* 26 C.F.R. § 54.4980H-3(c)(4)(ii).

Advantages of the Monthly Measurement Method

The monthly measurement method is best suited for employers who do not have a significant number of employees whose hours per week fluctuate above and below 30. Employers who have numerous employees with fluctuating hours or who have a large number of seasonal employees will likely prefer the look-back measurement method, described below. The monthly measurement method works well for employers who have generally stable full-time and part-time schedules and who may occasionally hire a new employee whose hours will likely be at the cusp of eligibility for health coverage.

The Look-Back Measurement Method

The look-back measurement method is complex and uses distinct terminology. It is appropriate for employees whose hours will be variable on an ongoing basis. The ACA refers to such employees as *variable-hour employees*. Under the look-back method of measuring the hours of a variable-hour employee, an employer chooses a period of between 3 and 12 months to serve as its *standard measurement period*. For new employees, the first standard measurement period is called the *initial measurement period*. The employer records and then averages the number of hours of service per week each employee works during that measurement period. Both the initial measurement period and each standard measurement period are followed by a *stability period* during which an employee's status as full-time and eligible for health insurance or part-time and ineligible for health insurance is fixed. A stability period must be at least six months long and cannot be shorter than the standard measurement period that preceded it. The cycle of measurement period followed by stability period repeats continuously until an employee separates from service.[20]

An employee who works an average of 30 hours per week during a standard measurement period must be treated as a full-time employee and offered health insurance coverage during the subsequent stability period, whether or not the employee actually works an average of 30 hours per week

20. *See* 26 C.F.R. §§ 54.4980H-1(a)(45), (46), and (49).

during the stability period.[21] If an employee does *not* work an average of 30 hours during a standard measurement period, then the employee may be treated as part-time during the subsequent stability period and need not be offered health insurance coverage. Because the employee will not be eligible for health insurance during the entirety of the stability period—even if that employee begins to regularly work more than 30 hours per week—the stability period cannot be longer than the standard measurement period that preceded it.[22]

A stability period will necessarily overlap to some extent with a new standard measurement period. This means that if an employee who is treated as full-time during a stability period (because that employee worked an average of 30 hours per week during the preceding measurement period) does not actually work 30 hours per week during the stability period, the employee need not be treated as full-time during the next stability period and will not have to be offered health insurance coverage then. Similarly, if an employee who is not treated as full-time during a stability period (because that employee did not work an average of 30 hours per week during the preceding measurement period) does in fact work an average of 30 hours per week or more during the stability period, that employee will be considered full-time during the next stability period and should be offered health insurance coverage.

Similarly, an employee who starts a stability period as a full-time employee but experiences a reduction in hours such that the employee no longer averages 30 hours of service per week continues to be treated as a full-time employee covered by health insurance until the end of that stability period.

An employee who starts a stability period as a part-time employee working an average of fewer than 30 hours per week and experiences an increase in hours of service during the stability period remains a part-time employee for ACA purposes until the start of the next stability period, at which time the employer must allow the employee to enroll in the employer's health plan.[23]

---

21. *See* 26 C.F.R. § 54.4980H-3(d)(1)(iii).
22. *See* 26 C.F.R. § 54.4980H-3(d)(1)(iv).
23. *See* 26 C.F.R. § 54.4980H-3(d)(1)(vii).

Optional Administrative Period

Employers may use an optional administrative period between the end of a standard measurement period and the beginning of a stability period. An administrative period cannot be longer than 90 days. Generally, the purpose of the administrative period is to give employers time to offer and enroll employees in health insurance coverage for the next stability period. The administrative period must overlap with the prior stability period so that any employee being treated as a full-time employee based on an earlier measurement period continues to be covered by health insurance until the start of the next stability period.[24]

For example:

> *Paradise County uses a standard measurement period that begins on October 15 of each year, a stability period that begins on January 1 of each year, and an administrative period that runs from October 15 to January 1 of each year. An employee who is treated as a full-time employee for the stability period beginning January 1, 2016, and running through December 31, 2016, will be offered health insurance for the entire period, even if the employee averages fewer than 30 hours per week during the period October 14, 2015, through October 13, 2016. The employee will continue to be covered through December 31, 2016, but the county will use the period from October 15–December 31, 2016, to advise the employee of his or her COBRA rights and effect disenrollment of the employee for the period beginning January 1, 2017.[25]*

Choosing a Standard Measurement Period

Employers can choose the months during which a standard measurement period runs. If an employer chooses a 12-month or yearly measurement period, it may have the year begin on January 1, July 1, May 15, November 15, or on any other day so long as the standard measurement period is the same for all employees in the same category.[26] Different standard measurement periods and different stability periods may be designated for salaried employees and for hourly employees. The employer mandate regulations do

---

24. *See* 26 C.F.R. § 54.4980H-3(d)(1)(vi).
25. *See* 26 C.F.R. § 54.4980H-3(d)(1)(viii) for an additional example.
26. *See* 26 C.F.R. § 54.4980H-3(d)(1).

not recognize any other distinctions for measurement and stability period purposes for non-unionized employees.[27]

Options for Employers Using Weekly or Bi-weekly Payroll Periods

Employers who use a weekly or bi-weekly payroll period may treat a standard measurement period as ending on the last day of the payroll period preceding the payroll period in which the date that would otherwise be the end of the measurement period falls, if the measurement period begins on the first day of the payroll period in which the date that would otherwise be the date on which the beginning of the measurement period falls. Employers with weekly or bi-weekly payrolls may also treat a standard measurement period as beginning on the first day of the payroll period that follows the payroll period in which the date that would otherwise be the date on which the beginning of the measurement period falls, if the measurement period ends on the last day of the payroll period in which the date that would otherwise be the date on which the end of the measurement period falls.[28]

Treatment of New Employees under the Look-Back Measurement Method

As discussed above, new employees whom an employer reasonably expects to work an average of 30 hours per week must be offered affordable health coverage no later than the first day of the fourth full calendar month of employment. For new employees with variable hours, new seasonal employees, and new part-time employees who may or may not average 30 hours, employers may use the look-back method to determine whether the employee must be offered health coverage. To do so, employers measure the average hours of service by using an initial measurement period of between 3 and 12 consecutive months that begins either on

- the employee's start date,
- any day up to and including the first day of the first calendar month following the employee's start date, or
- the first day of the first payroll period starting after the employee's start date.[29]

---

27. *See* 26 C.F.R. § 54.4980H-3(d)(1)(v)(C). Other distinctions are permitted in the case of employees subject to collective-bargaining agreements.

28. *See* 26 C.F.R. § 54.4980H-3(d)(1)(iii).

29. *See* 26 C.F.R. §§ 54.4980H-3(d)(3)(i) and (ii).

If the employee averages 30 hours of service per month, the employer must offer affordable coverage beginning with the first day of the first calendar month of the following stability period (regardless of whether there is an administrative period between the initial measurement period and the stability period).[30] If an employee does not work an average of 30 hours during the initial measurement period, then the employee may be treated as part-time during the following stability period and need not be offered health insurance coverage. The stability period cannot be longer than the initial measurement period that preceded it and cannot exceed the remainder of the first entire standard measurement period (plus any associated administrative period for which the new employee has been employed).[31]

An employee who is a full-time employee on his or her start date but experiences a reduction in hours such that she or he no longer averages 30 hours of service per week continues to be treated as a full-time employee covered by health insurance until the end of the stability period associated with the initial assessment period. An employee who is a variable-hour employee on his or her start date and experiences an increase in hours of service during the initial measurement period such that the employer should reasonably expect that employee to average at least 30 hours of service must be offered health insurance coverage by the first day of the fourth full calendar month following the change in employment status.[32]

Choosing a stability period for new employees. The stability period that follows an initial measurement period must be the same length as the stability period for ongoing employees—namely, at least six months long and no shorter than the measurement period that preceded it.[33] As is the case with ongoing employees, different initial measurement periods and different stability periods may be designated for salaried employees and for hourly employees. The regulations do not recognize any other distinctions for measurement and stability period purposes.[34]

Choosing an administrative period for new employees. As is the case with ongoing employees, employers may use an optional administrative period

30. *See* 26 C.F.R. § 54.4980H-3(d)(3).

31. *See* 26 C.F.R. § 54.4980H-3(d)(3)(iv).

32. *See* 26 C.F.R. § 54.4980H-3(d)(3)(vii)(A).

33. *See* 26 C.F.R. §§ 54.4980H-3(d)(3)(i) and (iii).

34. *See* 26 C.F.R. § 54.4980H-3(d)(3)(v). Other distinctions are permitted in the case of employees subject to collective-bargaining agreements.

between the end of the initial measurement period and the beginning of a new employee's stability period. The administrative period cannot be longer than 90 days in total. In other words, the 90-day maximum includes all days between an employee's start date and the day on which he or she begins health care coverage, less the number of days in the initial measurement period. For example, if a new variable-hour employee began work on November 15, but the employer did not begin the initial measurement period until December 1, the sixteen days from November 15–30 would count against the 90-day administrative period maximum, and the maximum amount of time the administrative period that followed the initial measurement period could run would be 74 days.[35]

In addition, the combined initial measurement period and administrative period for a new employee cannot extend beyond the last day of the first calendar month beginning on or after the first anniversary of the employee's start date (in other words, it can never last more than 13 months under any circumstances).[36]

Transition from New Variable-Hour Employee to Ongoing Variable-Hour Employee

Once a new employee has been employed for an entire initial measurement period, the employer must begin testing the employee for full-time status at the same time as it does ongoing variable-hour employees, beginning with the standard measurement period currently running.

Take the following example.

> New variable-hour employee A works for an employer who uses a one-year initial measurement period that begins on an employee's first day of work and a calendar-year assessment period for ongoing employees. The employee began work on November 15, 2016. The initial measurement period runs through November 14, 2017. On November 15, 2017, the employer would measure the employee's hours to see if the employee averaged 30 hours per week during the preceding year. On January 1, 2018, the employer would measure the hours of its ongoing employees to see if they averaged 30 hours per week during the 2017 calendar year. It would, at that same time,

---

35. *See* 26 C.F.R. § 54.4980H-3(d)(3)(vi)(A).
36. *See* 26 C.F.R. § 54.4980H-3(d)(3)(vi)(B).

measure A's hours for the period January 1, 2017–December 31, 2017, to determine whether A averaged 30 hours per week during the 2017 calendar year.

If A averaged 30 hours per week during the initial assessment period ending on November 14, 2017, the employer would have to offer A health insurance coverage beginning on November 15, 2017, and lasting for a stability period of at least a year (until November 15, 2018) or until the beginning of the stability period associated with the first full standard measurement period after the employee's start date (until January 1, 2018), whichever is later. If A averages 30 hours per week during the first full standard measurement period (January 1, 2018–December 31, 2018), then A's health insurance coverage will continue through the stability period beginning on January 1, 2019. If for some reason A's average number of hours per week falls below 30 for the first standard measurement period, then A's health insurance coverage will cease as of January 1, 2019.[37]

Seasonal and Part-Time Employees

The same rules that apply to variable-hour employees apply to seasonal and part-time employees. If an employer has a one-year initial assessment period that begins on the employee's first day, and Lisa the Lifeguard begins work on May 15, 2017, Lisa's initial assessment period will run until May 14, 2018. The employer town, however, no longer stations lifeguards on its beaches after October 1, which is when Lisa's employment ends. The ACA defines a *seasonal employee* (as opposed to a seasonal worker) as one who is hired into a position for which the customary annual employment is six months or less.[38] Lisa the Lifeguard is a seasonal employee during the initial assessment period, does not end up averaging 30 hours per week during that time, and is no longer an employee when the initial assessment period ends and the stability period begins.[39]

Let's look at a few variations of this hypothetical. Even though the ACA defines a seasonal employee as one hired for less than 6 months of the year, assume that the City of Paradise has a fancy pool with a retractable dome, and Lisa the Lifeguard's seasonal position runs for 38 weeks, a little less

---

37. *See* 26 C.F.R. § 54.4980H-3(d)(4).
38. *See* 26 C.F.R. § 54.4980H-1(a)(38).
39. *See* 26 C.F.R. § 54.4980H-3(d)(5) (Example 11).

than 8 months. Assume that Lisa works 40 hours per week for the full 38 weeks and that the city uses a look-back period of 12 months. Lisa the Lifeguard would then work 40 hours per week × 38 weeks or 1,520 hours in the 12-month look-back period. Then 1,520 is divided by 52 weeks of the year to equal an average of 29.23 hours per week, and this total squeaks in under the 30-hours-per-week dividing line between full-time and part-time status under the ACA. The city would not be obligated to offer health insurance to Lisa.

Now let's assume that Lisa the Lifeguard works 40 hours per week for 24 weeks, approximately 6 months and 10 hours per week in a different position for a second 24-week period. Lisa would work 960 hours in the first 24-week period and 240 hours in the second 24-week period for a total of 1,200 hours in 12 months. 1,200 divided by 52 weeks of the year equals an average of approximately 23 hours per week. The city would not be obligated to offer health insurance to Lisa.

Let's take another example. Stan's position as "Seasonal Assistant to the Parks and Recreation Director" is a jack-of-all-trades position for the town of Amazing Beach. Stan is employed for six months, from May 15 through October 15. He helps out whenever and wherever needed during the busy summer months and frequently works 60–70 hours per week. Stan's employer uses an initial 6-month measurement period and Stan averages 30 hours per week, entitling him to an offer of health coverage. Nevertheless, the town does not have to offer Stan health insurance, because at the end of six months, Stan no longer works for the town. An employer never has to offer coverage to an individual who is no longer employed.

Generally, an employer who has seasonal employees who work close to 6 months of the year will have to use a 12-month measurement period to show that they are not full-time employees and do not have to be offered health coverage. The ACA permits employers to have different measurement periods for salaried and non-salaried workers, but outside of this exception, an employer must use measurement periods of the same length for all employees. So any employer will have to use a 12-month measurement period for all employees to bring seasonal employees in under full-time (unless all of the seasonal employees are non-salaried, in which case the employer would have to use a 12-month measurement period for non-salaried employees, but could use a measurement period of a different length for salaried employees). If the seasonal employees work fewer than 6 months, an employer can probably use a shorter measurement period.

Treatment of Employees Rehired after Termination or Leave of Absence

A local government employee who did not have any hours of service for 13 consecutive weeks or more may be treated as a new employee for the purpose of determining hours of service.[40] For university, four-year college, community college, and public school employers, an employee who did not have any hours of service for 26 consecutive weeks or more may be treated as a new employee for the purpose of determining hours of service.[41]

A continuing employee—one who has not had any hours of service for a period of fewer than 13 weeks (or 26 weeks, if at an educational institution)—retains the status of full-time or part-time for the remainder of the stability period during which the leave occurred and must be offered resumption of coverage by no later than the first full day of the calendar month following the day on which the employee returned to work.[42] In using the look-back method to measure the hours of service of a continuing employee who has been on special unpaid leave, an employer must either (1) exclude the period of unpaid leave from the computation of the average number of hours for that measurement period and use the resulting average as the average for the entire measurement period or (2) credit the employee with the same average number of hours for the weeks of special unpaid leave as the employee had been averaging in the weeks preceding the leave. This is true for both local government and educational employers.[43]

Timing of the Offer of Coverage

The Basic Rules

New employees who an employer reasonably expects to work an average of 30 hours per week must be offered affordable health coverage no later than the first day of the fourth full calendar month of employment.[44] For those new employees whose average hours per week an employer cannot predict with certainty at the start of employment, the rule varies depending on whether the employer is using the monthly measurement period or the

---

40. *See* 26 C.F.R. § 54.4980H-3(d)(6)(i).
41. *See* 26 C.F.R. § 54.4980H-3(d)(6)(ii).
42. *See* 26 C.F.R. § 54.4980H-3(d)(6)(iii).
43. *See* 26 C.F.R. §§ 54.4980H-3(d)(6)(i)(B) and (d)(6)(ii)(B).
44. *See* 26 C.F.R. §§ 54.4980H-3(c)(2) and (d)(2)(iii).

look-back measurement period to determine eligibility for health insurance coverage.

- Under the monthly measurement method, if an employee averages 30 hours of service per week in any month, the employer must offer coverage beginning with the first day of the first calendar month following a three-month period beginning with the first full calendar month in which the employee averages 30 hours a week.[45] For example, if an employee begins work on November 15, the employer would begin to count that employee's hours on December 1 and, assuming that the employee averages 30 hours of service per week in December, the employer must offer that employee health insurance coverage effective the following March 1. But what if the employee averages fewer than 30 hours of service per week during January and February? An employer who finds that employees who average 30 hours per week in the first month or two of the monthly measurement period but then work fewer than 30 in subsequent months should switch to using the look-back measurement period. Under the monthly measurement method, once an employee first averages 30 hours in a month, the employer must make an offer of coverage.
- Under the look-back measurement method, if a variable-hour, seasonal, or part-time employee averages 30 hours of service per month during the initial measurement period or in any subsequent measurement period, an employer must offer coverage beginning with the first day of the first calendar month of the following stability period and any associated administrative period.[46]

Waiting and Orientation Periods under the Affordable Care Act

The ACA allows employers to require a waiting period of up to 90 days before an otherwise eligible employee begins coverage under the employer's group health plan. The concept of "otherwise eligible" refers to requirements the employer may impose for an employee to participate in the employer's health insurance plan, such as being in a particular job classification (for

---

45. *See* 26 C.F.R. §§ 54.4980H-3(c)(1) and (2) and the discussion of the monthly measurement method above on pages 55–58.

46. *See* 26 C.F.R. § 54.4980H-3(d)(3).

example, all administrative or management employees, or all public safety employees), working a certain number of hours per week, satisfying all licensure requirements for the position, or completing a probationary period. Once a new employee satisfies all the requirements to participate in the health plan, he or she cannot be required to wait more than 90 calendar days (including weekends and holidays) after the date upon which the employee satisfies the prerequisites to enroll in the health plan.[47]

Measurement Periods for Variable-Hour Employees and the 90-Day Waiting Period

When an employer uses the look-back measurement method to determine whether a newly hired employee is working an average of 30 hours per week, it is permitted to use an initial measurement period of up to 12 months. An employer may not, however, tack on a 90-day waiting period to a 12-month look-back measurement period. An employer must make an offer of coverage effective no later than 13 months from the employee's start date, unless the employee's start date was not the first day of the month, in which case coverage may begin the first day of the next calendar month.[48]

Cumulative Hours of Service Requirements

When it is unclear at the time of hire that an employee will be working an average of 30 hours per week, an employer may impose a requirement that a new employee complete a specified number of hours of service in order to become eligible to participate in its group health insurance plan. In such a case, the waiting period would not begin until the employee had worked the required number of hours and fulfilled that prerequisite to eligibility. The rules limit the number of cumulative hours of service an employer may require as a condition of eligibility to 1,200.[49]

---

47. *See* 26 C.F.R. §§ 54.9815-2708(a)–(c); 29 C.F.R. §§ 2590.715-2708(a)–(c); 45 C.F.R. §§ 147.116(a)–(c).

48. *See* 26 C.F.R. § 54.9815-2708(c)(3)(i); 29 C.F.R. § 2590.715-2708(c)(3)(i); 45 C.F.R. § 147.116(c)(3)(i).

49. *See* 26 C.F.R. § 54.9815-2708(c)(3)(ii); 29 C.F.R. § 2590.715-2708(c)(3)(ii); 45 C.F.R. § 147.116 (c)(3)(ii).

Orientation (Probationary) Periods

The ACA regulations refer to what many public employers call probationary periods as "orientation periods." These are initial periods of work during which the employee undergoes any needed orientation or training and the employer evaluates whether the employee seems likely to be able to do the job successfully. Under the ACA regulations, employers may adopt an orientation period of no longer than one month as part of the process of an employee's becoming otherwise eligible for participating in an employer's group health plan. In other words, an employer may require a one-month probationary period before determining that an employee will continue in employment and is otherwise eligible for health insurance. The 90-day waiting period would then begin on the first day after the conclusion of the one-month orientation period.[50]

Measuring the one-month orientation period. Because months are of different lengths, the rules provide that for orientation period purposes, a month is to be measured as one calendar month minus one calendar day from the employee's start date in a position otherwise eligible for coverage. Where the month in which the start date falls is longer than the following month, the one month is measured as the last day of the following month. Thus, for an employee beginning work on January 30 or 31, the one-month orientation period will end on February 28 (29 in a leap year).[51]

Intersection of a waiting or orientation period with the no-coverage penalty. In most cases, use of a one-month orientation period followed by a 90-day waiting period will result in an employee's beginning health insurance coverage on the first day of the fourth month of employment as a full-time employee, and the employer will not be liable for the no-coverage penalty. However, the first day of the fourth month of employment can fall before the date that corresponds to one month of orientation plus 90 days of waiting. In that case, there is no exemption for the employer, who would be liable for the no-coverage penalty for that month.[52]

---

50. *See* 26 C.F.R. § 54.9815-2708(c)(3)(iii).

51. *See* 26 C.F.R. § 54.9815-2708(c)(3)(iii).

52. *See* 26 C.F.R. §§ 54.9815-2708(c)(3)(iii) and (f) (Example 11); 29 C.F.R. §§ 2590.715-2708(c)(3)(iii) and (f) (Example 11); and 45 C.F.R. §§ 147.116(c)(3)(iii) and (f) (Example 11).

Part 4

The Affordable Care Act and Health Reimbursement Accounts, Health Savings Accounts, Flexible Spending Accounts, Employer Payment Plans, and Employee Assistance Programs

Health reimbursement accounts (HRAs), health savings accounts (HSAs), health flexible spending accounts (FSAs), employer payment plans (EPPs) (whereby an employer deducts amounts from an employee's wages on a pre-tax basis and uses the money to pay for health insurance premiums), and employee assistance programs (EAPs) all qualify as employer-sponsored group health insurance plans under the Affordable Care Act (ACA).[1] Thus, they are all subject to the rule prohibiting group health plans from establishing any annual dollar limits on essential benefits and the rule prohibiting cost-sharing for preventative health services. As a direct result of their status as health plans, the rules governing HRAs, HSAs, FSAs, EPPs, and even EAPs have changed, in some cases dramatically, in others less so. The impact of the ACA on each of these arrangements is outlined below.

Health Reimbursement Accounts

A health reimbursement arrangement, sometimes called a health reimbursement account, is a tax-favored employer-sponsored plan through which employees and retirees may be reimbursed for qualified medical expenses for themselves, their spouses, dependents, and children younger

---

1. *See* 42 U.S.C. § 18021(b)(3); 42 U.S.C. § 300gg-91(a).

than age 26. HRAs are funded solely by employer contributions, which are excludable from employees' gross income for tax purposes. Unlike contributions to a flexible spending account (FSA), money that accumulates in an HRA may be carried over from year to year and funds contributed to the account in one year may be used to reimburse expenses incurred in a later year. Funds may never be used for anything but qualified medical expenses, as they are defined in Section 213(d) of the Internal Revenue Code. For an HRA, qualified medical expenses include health insurance premiums, co-payments and co-insurance, and deductibles. HRA contributions may not be used to pay for essential health benefits.[2] HRAs may also be used to purchase health plans for excepted benefits such as vision or dental care that are purchased in the individual market.[3] There are no contribution limits on an HRA other than what an employer is willing to contribute on a yearly basis. The employer may, however, establish maximum reimbursement amounts for any coverage period.[4]

Because a health reimbursement arrangement cannot meet the requirement that there be no lifetime or annual dollar limits on essential health benefits, or the requirement that there be no cost-sharing on preventative health measures, an employer may not establish an HRA in place of offering a traditional health insurance plan. It may establish an HRA only *in addition* to sponsoring a group health plan. In other words, HRAs are generally lawful only where the employer limits their availability to employees who are also covered by an employer group health plan that has no annual dollar limits

---

2. *See* Internal Revenue Service, Notice 2013-54, *Application of Market Reform and Other Provisions of the Affordable Care Act to HRAs, Health FSAs, and Certain Other Employer Healthcare Arrangements* (hereinafter *Application of Market Reform and Other Provisions of the Affordable Care Act*), https://www.irs.gov/pub/irs-drop/n-13-54.pdf.

3. *See* Internal Revenue Service, Notice 2015-87, *Further Guidance on the Application of the Group Health Plan Market Reform Provisions of the Affordable Care Act to Employer-Provided Health Coverage and on Certain Other Affordable Care Act Provisions* (hereinafter, *Further Guidance on the Application of the Group Health Plan Market Reform Provisions*), https://www.irs.gov/pub/irs-drop/n-15-87.pdf, at Q&A 5.

4. *See Further Guidance on the Application of the Group Health Plan Market Reform Provisions*; *Application of Market Reform and Other Provisions of the Affordable Care Act*; Internal Revenue Service, Notice 2002-45, *Health Reimbursement Arrangements*, https://www.irs.gov/pub/irs-drop/n-02-45.pdf; Internal Revenue Service, Revenue Ruling 2002-41, https://www.irs.gov/pub/irs-drop/rr-02-41.pdf.

on essential health benefits and provides minimum value.[5] Once a current employee ceases to be covered by the employer's health plan, the funds in the HRA may no longer be used. They are forfeited.[6] HRAs may be used to cover the qualified medical expenses of spouses, dependents, and children only when they are also enrolled in the employer's health plan.[7]

Because a free-standing HRA may no longer lawfully be established, HRAs cannot be used to fund employee purchases of plans on the individual market—other than plans providing excepted benefits such as vision, dental, or cancer care. This is true both for covered employers and for small employers not subject to the ACA.

The amount contributed to employee HRAs in a given year may be used to determine whether the employer's health plan is affordable and offers minimum value.[8] For a discussion of how to report contributions to an HRA to employees and the Internal Revenue Service (IRS) on Forms 1094 and 1095, see below, pages 106–107.

As a practical matter, an HRA must either allow employees to forfeit their rights to any balances in their HRA accounts once their medical coverage under that employer plan ends or give employees the opportunity to waive their rights in their account balances on an annual basis. This is because as long as an employee has an HRA account balance, the IRS will consider that employee to have minimum essential coverage through the employer.[9] An employee who has minimum essential coverage may not apply for a premium tax credit from the government. This could pose a

---

5. *See Further Guidance on the Application of the Group Health Plan Market Reform Provisions* and *Application of Market Reform and Other Provisions of the Affordable Care Act.*

6. *See Further Guidance on the Application of the Group Health Plan Market Reform Provisions,* at Q&A 2.

7. *See Further Guidance on the Application of the Group Health Plan Market Reform Provisions,* at Q&A 4; *Application of Market Reform and Other Provisions of the Affordable Care Act.*

8. *See Application of Market Reform and Other Provisions of the Affordable Care Act,* Section 4.

9. *See* the discussion of minimum essential coverage (MEC) above on page 32. Unused amounts in an HRA credited before January 1, 2014, may continue to be used to reimburse medical expenses in accordance with the terms of the HRA as then existed, even if that use would otherwise cause the HRA to fail to comply with the annual dollar limit prohibition and the preventative service requirements. *See Application of Market Reform and Other Provisions of the Affordable Care Act.*

significant hardship on an employee whose hours are reduced or who elects to go from full- to part-time status.

HRAs and Retirees

Under the ACA, HRAs can be used as a stand-alone plan for retiree benefits without the retirees having to be enrolled in a group health plan, because a retiree-only plan is considered an excepted benefit and is therefore not subject to ACA requirements. Nevertheless, retiree-only HRAs must also allow participants to waive their rights to their account balances on a yearly basis.

Health Savings Accounts

Health savings accounts (HSAs) allow employees to accumulate funds on a pre-tax basis to pay for specific types of medical expenses, including health insurance co-payments and deductibles. HSAs may be established, however, only in conjunction with a specific form of health insurance plan—a high-deductible health insurance plan (HDHP). An HDHP is defined by the Internal Revenue Code as a health plan having for 2017 (1) an annual deductible of at least $1,300 for individual coverage and at least $2,600 for family coverage and (2) a cap of $6,550 or less on the annual total amount paid by an individual for the deductible and any other out-of-pocket expenses (not including premiums) and a cap of $13,100 or less on the annual total amount paid under family coverage for the deductible and any out-of-pocket expenses.[10] The Internal Revenue Service updates these figures each year. The high-deductible plan may take the form of a traditional major medical indemnity plan, a health maintenance organization (HMO), or a preferred provider plan (PPO). Self-insured local government employers may offer HSAs so long as the self-insured health plan meets the definition of an HDHP.

In contrast to HRAs, the IRS does not consider HSAs to be health plans offering minimum essential coverage (MEC). Because employer reporting to the IRS on Forms 1094 and 1095 is designed to give the IRS information about which individuals have MEC and whether they have received offers of

---

10. *See* Internal Revenue Service, Rev. Proc. 2016-28, https://www.irs.gov/pub/irs-drop/rp-16-28.pdf.

MEC from their employers, employers do not have to file annual information reports about HSAs either to the IRS or to employees.

Health Flexible Savings Arrangements

Health care flexible spending accounts (FSAs) are employer-maintained accounts into which employees contribute a percentage of their salary pretax for use in paying unreimbursed medical expenses up to a maximum of $2,500 for a given calendar year. Employers may also make contributions to FSAs on their employees' behalf, but this is not common in local government. Because employees typically use health FSAs to pay non-reimbursed medical expenses like deductibles, the Internal Revenue Service has always considered FSAs to be *health plans* that pay "first-dollar expenses."

Rules prohibiting annual dollar limits do not apply to health FSAs, provided that the FSA is offered as part of an IRS Code Section 125 cafeteria plan.[11] To be exempt from the ACA's preventative services requirement, health FSAs must conform to one of two models. They must be offered as part of a Section 125 cafeteria plan, and either (1) literally provide only "excepted benefits," such as stand-alone dental or vision benefits or (2) be integrated with an employer-sponsored group health plan. The IRS considers an FSA to be one that provides only excepted benefits if it is offered in conjunction with a group health plan that provides coverage other than excepted benefits and the maximum benefit available to any participant through the FSA does not exceed two times the employee's salary reduction for the FSA for the year or $500 plus the amount of the salary reduction (elsewhere, the ACA limits the annual salary reduction for health FSAs to $2,600).[12] In other words, only employees who are eligible to participate in the employer's group health plan may establish an FSA. This does not mean that the employee has to elect coverage under the plan, only that he or she has the ability to do so. Part-time employees (or any other categories of employee) who are not eligible for employer-sponsored health insurance cannot elect a pre-tax deduction from salary into an FSA.

---

11. *See Application of Market Reform and Other Provisions of the Affordable Care Act*, esp. at Q&A 8; 26 C.F.R. § 54.9815-2711T(a)(2)(ii).

12. *See Application of Market Reform and Other Provisions of the Affordable Care Act*, esp. at Q&A 7; 26 C.F.R. § 54.9831-1(c)(3)(v).

Employer Payment Plans: Funding Employee Purchases of Individual Plans on the Individual Market

An employer payment plan is any arrangement whereby an employer facilitates an employee's purchase of health insurance using pre-tax dollars. A health FSA offered through an IRS Section 125 cafeteria plan is an employer payment plan. The IRS has clarified in Notice 2013-54 that employers cannot pay for individual health insurance policies bought through the Exchange or on the open market with pre-tax dollars, whether the employer pays for those policies directly or through pre-tax salary deductions. According to the IRS, such a practice violates the ACA's prohibition on annual dollar limits on essential health benefits and the requirement that non-grandfathered plans provide first dollar coverage of preventative services.[13]

An employer may pay employees higher salaries to facilitate their purchase of individual health insurance policies. An employer may even deduct the cost of an individual premium and make payment to a health insurer on the employee's behalf on an after-tax basis, so long as the employer neither endorses nor limits the employee's choices on the Exchange or open market.[14]

Penalties for Improper Use of an HRA, an HSA, or a Health FSA

Violation of the ACA rules governing the use of HRAs, HSAs, and health FSAs will subject an employer to a tax of $100 per day per individual employee—a steep penalty.[15]

Employee Assistance Programs

Final regulations on employee assistance programs (EAPs) have not been issued. The IRS has said that for the moment it will not treat EAPs as group health plans, but will instead consider them "excepted benefits" not sub-

---

13. *See Application of Market Reform and Other Provisions of the Affordable Care Act.*

14. *See Application of Market Reform and Other Provisions of the Affordable Care Act.*

15. *See* 26 U.S.C. § 4980D(b)(1).

ject to rules concerning cost-sharing and essential benefits, provided that the EAP does not provide significant medical benefits.[16] What are significant medical benefits? Employers are told to use a "reasonable, good faith interpretation" of the phrase.[17] Presumably, an average EAP—one where the benefits are not better than most—would not be considered a group health plan and an EAP that offered noticeably richer benefits than most might be. Employers are advised to work closely with and ask questions of the consultants they use to develop EAP programs.

---

16. *See Application of Market Reform and Other Provisions of the Affordable Care Act*, at Q&A 9.

17. *See Application of Market Reform and Other Provisions of the Affordable Care Act*, at Q&A 9.

Part 5

The Affordable Care Act's Reporting Requirements

As Part I discussed in greater detail, the Affordable Care Act (ACA) requires larger employers (those with 50 or more full-time equivalent employees) to offer insurance that provides minimum essential coverage to their full-time employees, or pay either a penalty for failure to offer coverage (the "no-coverage" penalty) or a penalty for failure to offer affordable coverage that provides minimum value (the "inadequate-coverage" penalty). That is the *employer mandate.* The ACA also requires virtually all individuals to secure health insurance that provides minimum essential coverage, or pay a penalty. That is the *individual mandate.* To help individuals meet this mandate, the federal government has set up online health insurance exchanges designed to make it simpler for individuals who do not get health insurance coverage through their employment to purchase it. Together, these mandates make up *shared responsibility* for ensuring that individuals have health insurance coverage—an obligation that rests both with individuals and with employers that have at least 50 full-time equivalent employees.

What is minimum essential coverage? As discussed in greater detail in Part 1, the accurate but non-helpful answer is that it allows an individual to meet his or her responsibility to acquire coverage and is the kind of coverage larger employers must offer to their employees. The practical answer is that the kinds of coverage insurers may offer on the health insurance exchanges for individual purchase and the kinds of coverage employers may offer to their employees through insurance contracts or by self-insuring both qualify as minimum essential coverage, as does COBRA coverage. Medicare and

Medicare Advantage plans also qualify. If an employer offers coverage that meets the requirements on coverage imposed by the ACA, it is offering minimum essential coverage. In a few cases, even employer-sponsored coverage that does not meet all the requirements imposed by the ACA is still considered to provide minimum essential coverage if the plan is a "grandfathered plan."

Tracking the Employer Mandate

The federal government needs to know which employers are meeting their obligation to offer minimum essential coverage to full-time employees and which are not. With that knowledge, it can determine which employers must pay the penalty for failure to offer the required coverage. How does the federal government know whether an employer is meeting this obligation? It requires employers to report to the Internal Revenue Service (IRS)—and to individual employees—particulars of offers of coverage to individual employees. That is, the employer must tell the IRS about its offers of coverage to every full-time employee on a month-to-month basis. This is known as the "6056" reporting requirement, after the relevant Internal Revenue Code section. It contrasts with the "6055" individual mandate reporting discussed later. The two are easily confused since the numbers are so similar.

Who Must Report the 6056 Employer Mandate Offer-of-Coverage Information?

Every employer with 50 or more full-time equivalent employees must offer to its full-time employees minimum essential coverage and must report that offer of coverage to the IRS and to the employees themselves.

As anyone who has been through the exercise can attest, determining whether an employer has 50 or more full-time equivalent employees (and so is covered by the employer mandate) and which employees are full-time employees for purposes of the ACA and thus entitled to an offer of coverage is not necessarily easy. Figuring out those questions is the subject of Part 1 of this book and of a University of North Carolina at Chapel Hill School of Government webinar-on-demand.[1]

---

1. Diane M. Juffras, *The Affordable Care Act Webinar-on-Demand* (School of Government, University of North Carolina at Chapel Hill), https://www.sog.unc.edu/

How Is the 6056 Employer Mandate
Offer-of-Coverage Information Reported?

Employers with 50 or more full-time equivalent employees will report their offer-of-coverage information using Forms 1094-C and 1095-C. An employer files both forms with the IRS (just one Form 1094-C for all employees covered under the employer's plan and lots of Forms 1095-C—one for each individual employee). It also provides to each employee a Form 1095-C with information about just that employee. How to fill out Forms 1094-C and 1095-C is discussed later in this Part.

This basic reporting requirement has one important caveat. *If an employer with fewer than 50* full-time equivalent employees offers minimum essential coverage to its employees (even though the ACA does not require it to do so) through a self-insured plan, it must report that information to the IRS and to its employees to fulfill its 6055 (as opposed to 6056) reporting requirement as the entity providing minimum essential coverage. That 6055 reporting obligation is typically met through reporting on Forms 1094-B and 1095-B, and the under-50 employer may report that way, or it may choose to report using Forms 1094-C and 1095-C as if it were a larger employer covered by the employer mandate.

Tracking the Individual Mandate

The federal government needs to know which individuals have minimum essential coverage and which do not. With that knowledge, it can determine who must pay the penalty for failure to secure coverage and which individuals may qualify for a tax credit to help them afford the required coverage.

How does the federal government know whether individuals have coverage? It will gather that information in two ways. First, it will ask each individual who files an income tax return with the IRS whether that individual had coverage for every month of the year. This is the **Line 61** question on IRS Form 1040, U.S. Individual Income Tax Return. If the answer is "yes," that's the end of the inquiry. If the answer is "no," the individual must turn to another form to determine the amount of the penalty, if any, or whether a tax credit is available.

---

courses/webinars/affordable-health-care-act-webinar-demand#!/.

Second, the IRS knows that not every individual will answer the Line 61 question correctly—some individuals may not be truthful and others may simply not understand what is being asked. For that reason, the IRS requires that every *provider of minimum essential coverage* for every individual in the country must report that information to the IRS and to the individuals themselves. This is the "6055" reporting requirement, after the relevant Internal Revenue Code section.

Who Must Report the 6055 Individual Mandate Coverage Information?

The short answer is: Anyone who provides minimum essential coverage to any individual. For employers who offer their employees fully insured plans (plans offered under contract with an insurance carrier), the insurance carrier will file the 6055 individual mandate coverage reports. *Employers who offer minimum essential coverage to their employees through a self-insured plan (perhaps using a third party administrator but not involving an insurance contract with an insurance carrier) have the responsibility to report the 6055 individual mandate coverage.*

How Is the 6055 Individual Mandate Coverage Information Reported?

How Section 6055 individual mandate coverage information is reported to the IRS depends on whether the insurance company is reporting (because the employer is offering a fully insured plan) or the employer is reporting (because the employer is offering a self-insured plan).

Where the obligation rests with the insurance company to report the 6055 minimum essential coverage information, it will report that information by using Forms 1094-B and 1095-B. It files both forms with the IRS (just one 1094-B for all employees covered under the employer's plan and lots of 1095-Bs—one for each individual employee). It also provides a Form 1095-B to each employee.

Where the obligation rests with the employer to report the 6055 individual mandate coverage information, it may choose to file the information on Forms 1094-B and 1095-B in the same way an insurance company would. However, because the employer must report information on each employee under the employer's Section 6056 reporting requirement anyway, the IRS allows employers to file 6055 individual mandate coverage information in Part III of Form 1095-C, and not file Forms 1094-B and 1095-B at all. The IRS and the employee will get the relevant information through the C forms filings.

Overview of Reporting Requirements for Small Employers

- Under 50 full-time equivalent employees (FTEs) and offer no coverage: no reporting requirement
- Under 50 FTEs but offer coverage through a fully insured plan: no reporting requirement (but the insurer will report on Forms 1094-B and 1095-B)
- Under 50 FTEs but offer a self-insured plan: reporting requirement the same as a covered larger employer

Managing the Reporting Obligation

The obligation imposed on employers of 50 or more FTEs is significant. Employers must track, month-by-month, which employees are full-time employees entitled by law to an offer of minimum essential coverage and then must report that information to the IRS (and to the employees themselves) using Forms 1094-C and 1095-C.

How is an employer to manage this responsibility, especially the reporting obligation? It has three basic options. First, it can track all the relevant information in-house, using its own employees and tracking systems, and it can complete the forms in-house and report to the IRS and to employees itself. Second, it can track the relevant information itself and enter that information into reporting formats, but then engage a third party to report to the IRS and to employees, using the third party's software. That relieves the employer of the need to interface directly with the IRS, but it cannot, of course, relieve the employer of its ultimate obligation to see that the information is correctly reported. Third, the employer can contract with a third party to track the relevant information about employees, determine who is a full-time employee entitled to an offer of coverage for ACA purposes, accumulate the information into reporting formats, complete the forms, and report to the IRS and the employees. This alternative also does not relieve the employer of its potential liability for penalties if the information is incorrectly reported.

Overview of the Forms

Forms 1095-B and 1095-C report detailed substantive information, one form per individual employee or covered beneficiary of the employer health plan. Forms 1094-B and 1094-C are transmittal cover sheets reporting summary information about all of the individuals who are the subjects of Forms 1095-B and 1095-C. The B forms report summary information (1094-B) and detailed individual information (1095-B) that allows the IRS to track compliance with the individual mandate. The C forms report detailed information about which months of the year individual employees and their family members and dependents, where applicable, had health coverage or offers of health coverage that satisfied the individual mandate (1094-C) and the employer mandate (1095-C). The B forms are issued only by employers with a self-insured health plan. Employers who are fully insured by contracting with a health insurance company do not file the B forms—the health insurers themselves do. Examples of all of the forms appear in the appendixes.

Reporting for Employees in Limited Non-assessment Periods

Understanding the concept of the limited non-assessment period is crucial to successful completion of Forms 1094-C and 1095-C (the employer-mandate forms). A limited non-assessment period is a period of time during which an employee who works an average of 30 hours per week is not counted as a full-time employee for the purposes of assessing the no-coverage and the inadequate-coverage penalties. That same employee, however, would be counted as full-time for the purpose of determining whether an employer is an applicable large employer covered by the ACA. The guide to the forms found later in this part and the IRS Instructions for Forms 1094-C and 1095-C both instruct employers when not to count employees in limited non-assessment periods.

The most common limited non-assessment periods are as follows.

- *First calendar month of employment.* Employees who will clearly be full-time employees are in a limited non-assessment period during their first full month of employment if they have started work on any day other than the first of the month.
- *Waiting periods.* The ACA allows employers to require a waiting period of up to 90 days before an otherwise eligible employee (for example, an employee who has completed a probationary period) begins coverage under the employer's group health plan. Employees

who have not yet received an offer of coverage because they are in a waiting period are said to be in a limited non-assessment period and should not be counted as full-time employees for the purposes of the no-coverage or the inadequate-coverage penalty unless the employer is otherwise directed to do so. For a full discussion of waiting periods, see pages 66–68 above.

- *Initial measurement periods and any associated administrative period.* For employers using the look-back measurement method to determine whether a new variable-hour or seasonal employee is a full-time employee, the initial measurement period, whatever its length (which may be as little as 3 months or as many as 12 months), and any administrative period that follows are considered a limited non-assessment period during which employees should not be counted as full-time employees for the purposes of the employer mandate penalties. For a full discussion of initial measurement and administrative periods, see pages 58–64 above.

Form 1094-C (Transmittal for Form 1095-C)

Overview of Form 1094-C

An employer must file a Form 1094-C (transmittal form) whenever it files any Forms 1095-C (substantive employer mandate reporting form about individual employees). Forms 1095-C are filed in batches, so an employer may choose to file all Forms 1095-C with a single Form 1094-C or it may choose to file its Forms 1095-C by department—for example, with a Form 1094-C transmittal form for each department. An employer must, however, file one (and only one) Form 1094-C that contains all of the aggregated information for all of the Forms 1095-C filed by the employer. This is known as the *authoritative transmittal* and the individual form that is designated as the authoritative transmittal must be identified as such on **line 19** of Part 1 of Form 1094-C.

Line-by-Line Description of the Information Required by Form 1094-C

Local government employers will fill out **lines 1–8** of Form 1094-C. The information requested is, for the most part, self-explanatory, and includes the name of the employer and the employer tax identification number, among other things. **Lines 7 and 8** ask for the name of the person the IRS should contact if it has any questions and that person's phone number.

Many local government employers will be able to ignore **lines 9–16** and leave them blank. These lines are for use by governmental employers for whom another agency will do the reporting and primarily affect agencies of state and federal government.

Line 17 is reserved for IRS use.

In **line 18**, employers should enter the total number of Forms 1095-C that will be transmitted with this Form 1094-C. If an employer is filing its Forms 1095-C by department or some other grouping, it will have multiple Form 1094-C transmittal sheets and line 18 should show the number of Forms 1095-C being filed with this particular transmittal sheet.

In **line 19**, employers must indicate whether this particular transmittal sheet is the authoritative transmittal for that employer by checking the "yes" box. If an employer is using only one Form 1094-C transmittal sheet and is filing all of its Forms 1095-C together, it should answer "yes." If an employer is filing Forms 1095-C in batches, then one of the Forms 1094-C will be the authoritative transmittal, should be identified as such by marking the "yes" box, *and that form should contain aggregate information about **all** of the employer's employees, not just the employees in the batch being transmitted.* Employers should leave line 19 blank on all of the other Forms 1094-C, indicating that these are not authoritative transmittals containing data about all employees, and fill out the remainder of the forms with data summarizing what they are reporting in only those Forms 1095-C that accompany them.

Lines 20–22 should be filled out only if this particular Form 1094-C is the authoritative transmittal. Employers submitting Forms 1095-C in multiple batches should leave these lines blank on any additional Forms 1094-C that are not the authoritative transmittal.

On **line 20** of the Form 1094-C that is the authoritative transmittal, employers should enter the total number of individual Forms 1095-C it will be filing. This number should include both the number of Forms 1095-C filed with the authoritative transmittal and all other Forms 1095-C filed with other Form 1094-C transmittal sheets.

Local government employers will answer "no" to **line 21**. An aggregated applicable large employer (ALE) group is one where several separate organizations (usually private-sector companies) have a common owner or are otherwise related for purposes of the Internal Revenue Code. These organizations are generally combined and treated as a single employer for determining when an employer is covered by the ACA's employer mandate.

Line 22 asks the employer to certify whether it is eligible to use any of four reporting methods. Both the Qualifying Offer Method and the 98% Offer Method give an employer the opportunity to simplify some of the reporting it must do on the accompanying Forms 1095-C. Employers may check all methods of reporting for which it is eligible. For reporting information for calendar year 2016 only, there is an additional box employers may check called Section 4980H Transition Relief. This offers employers using non-calendar year plans the opportunity to reduce any penalties they might be assessed in conjunction with the 2016 months that fell within the 2015 plan year.

A *qualifying offer* is an offer of minimum essential coverage (MEC) (that is, employer-sponsored health coverage) that provides minimum value made to a full-time employee for whom a no-coverage or inadequate-coverage penalty could apply. The employee cost for employee-only coverage cannot exceed 9.5% (as adjusted upward annually) of the federal poverty line for single persons divided by 12, provided that the offer includes an offer of minimum essential coverage to the employee's spouse and dependents. In other words, a qualifying offer is an offer that meets all ACA requirements.

The *Qualifying Offer Method* itself is a simplified method of reporting information required by lines 14 and 15 of Form 1095-C. To use this simplified method, an employer must have made and must certify that it made a "qualifying offer" of coverage to one or more of its full-time employees for all of the months of the year in which an employee was one for whom a shared-responsibility penalty could apply by checking line 22, Box A, "Qualifying Offer Method." Information on how to report using the Qualifying Offer Method may be found in the section on Form 1095-C. In addition, employers eligible for the Qualifying Offer Method may provide alternate statements in place of Form 1095-C to employees who received qualifying offers for all twelve months of 2015. See the section on Alternate Method of Reporting to Employees for Form 1095-C, below on page 114.

The *98% Offer Method* is available to an employer who certifies that it offered affordable, minimum value health insurance for all of the months during which an employee was employed and not in a limited non-assessment period to 98% or more of those employees for whom it must file a Form 1095-C. The employer must also have made an offer of MEC to the employees' dependents. Employers using the 98% Offer Method do not have to identify which employees are full-time employees and are not required to complete Part III, lines 23–35, column (b), "Full-Time Employee Count for ALE Member."

Section 4980H Transition Relief (for 2015 plan years only) extends the transition relief offered to non-calendar year plans in calendar year 2015 to calendar year 2016. There are two types of transition relief, one for employers with 50–99 full-time employees and one for employers with 100 or more full-time employees. For employers with 50–99 employees who have a non-calendar year plan, neither no-coverage nor inadequate-coverage penalties will be assessed for any 2016 calendar month that falls within the 2015 plan year. For employers with 100 or more full-time employees who have a non-calendar year plan, any no-coverage penalty assessed for any 2016 calendar month that falls within the 2015 plan year will be calculated by reducing the employer's number of full-time employees by 80 rather than by the statutory 30. For a more detailed discussion of Section 4980H Transition Relief, see the section on Non-calendar Year Plan Transitional Relief for 2016 on pages 108–112.

Part III of Form 1094-C **(lines 23–35)** asks for month-by-month information about the numbers of employees receiving offers of health insurance coverage. **Line 23, column (a),** asks whether the employer offered minimum essential coverage (MEC) (in other words, its health insurance plan) to 95% of its full-time employees and their dependents for all 12 months of the reporting year. An employee in a limited non-assessment period should *not* be counted when calculating the number of full-time employees who received offers of coverage.

An employer who checks "no" in line 23, column (a), because it did not offer minimum essential coverage to 95% of its full-time employees and dependents for all 12 months of the year should continue down column (a), indicating for each month of the year **(lines 24–35)** whether it offered MEC to 95% of full-time employees and dependents in that month. This is the first clue to the IRS that a no-coverage penalty may apply.

In **column (b) of lines 23–35,** the employer should report the average number of full-time employees for the year. If the employer had exactly the same number of full-time employees each month of the reporting year, it should enter that number in **line 23, column (b).** If, as will be more often the case, the employer has had different numbers of full-time employees in different months of the year, the employer should enter the number of full-time employees for each month in **lines 24–35, column (b)**. Here, as in column (a), employers should *not* include employees in a limited non-assessment period when calculating the number of full-time employees for any month. The IRS does not require employers who indicate on line 22 that they are eligible to use the 98% Offer Method to complete column (b).

Column (c) of lines 23–35 asks employers to report the total number of employees, including full-time, part-time, *and* those in limited non-assessment periods that it has had each month of the reporting year. A full-time employee for this purpose is one who works an average of 30 hours per week. If the employer has had the exact same total number of employees each month of the year, it may enter that number in **line 23, column (c)**. If it has not, it should report the total number of employees it has had each month in **lines 24–35, column (c)**.

Employers must use a consistent method to count the number of employees. The IRS allows employers to choose among the following, provided that an employer uses the same method for each month of that reporting year:

- the first day of the month,
- the last day of the month,
- the first day of the first full payroll period of the month, or
- the last day of the first full payroll period of the month.

Local government employers should leave **column (d) of lines 23–35** blank as they will be not be members of an aggregated control group.

Relief for Non-calendar Year Plans

In 2016 only, employers with 50–99 FTEs who have non-calendar year plans will complete **column (e) of lines 23–35** of Form 1094-C. For 2016, the IRS is allowing employers with 50–99 employees who qualified for non-calendar year plan transition relief for 2015 to treat any employee and any dependents as having been offered coverage for those months in 2016 that were part of the 2015 calendar year. A fuller discussion of this provision may be found in *Section 4980H Transitional Relief for Non-calendar Year Plans for 2016 Only* on pages 108–109.

Local government employers do not need to fill out Part IV of the Form 1094-C transmittal sheet because they are not members of an aggregated applicable large employer group.

Form 1095-C

Overview of Form 1095-C

An employer must do two things with Form 1095-C. First, it must give to each full-time employee a copy of that employee's form. Second, it must file a copy of each employee's form with the IRS. One Form 1095-C must be filed for *each full-time employee* of an employer. Form 1095-C may only be used if the individual identified in line 1 has a Social Security number.

All local government employers—both those offering fully insured group health plans and those offering self-insured group health plans—must fill out and file a Form 1095-C for every employee to whom they have made an offer of coverage, whether or not the employee has accepted the offer and enrolled in employer-sponsored coverage. If an employer has made offers of coverage to 135 employees, it will have to file 135 individual Forms 1095-C. Dependents covered through an employee are listed on the same Form 1095-C as the employee.

Employers offering health insurance coverage through fully insured plans must fill out only Parts I and II. The information requested in Part III will be given to the IRS by the insurer. Self-insured employers must fill out Parts I, II, and III. The information requested in Part III is the same information requested of health insurance issuers in Form 1095-B. A self-insured employer who fills out Part III of Form 1095-C for a given employee does not have to issue Form 1095-B for that same employee.

Line-by-Line Description of the Information Required by Form 1095-C

Lines 1–6 of Form 1095-C are self-explanatory, asking for identifying information about the employee.

Lines 7–13 are equally self-explanatory, asking for identifying information about the reporting employer. **Line 10** asks for the telephone number of the person the employee may call for further information about what has been reported on Form 1095-C. This may or may not be the same person listed in Lines 7 and 8 of Form 1094-C, the contact for questions the IRS may have about the information reported in Form 1094-C, but since Form 1094-C reports aggregate information derived from the individual Forms 1095-C, it makes the most sense for the same person or office to be listed on both forms.

Social Security and Employer Identification Numbers on Forms

The IRS permits employers to truncate employee Social Security numbers on the forms given to the employees themselves by using asterisks (*) or the letter X for the first five numbers of the Social Security number and providing the correct last four numbers. The forms provided to the IRS, however, must include the full Social Security number. The full employer identification number must be provided on all forms given to both employees and the IRS without exception.

Part II, beginning with line 14, is where Form 1095-C becomes complicated. **Line 14** seeks information about offers of coverage that will help the IRS enforce the individual mandate. (Remember, each one of these Forms 1095-C is about a separate employee.) **Line 15** seeks information about the lowest-cost, employee-only premium amount an employee must contribute for coverage. This information will allow the IRS to determine whether that employee is eligible for a premium tax credit. **Line 16** seeks information about whether a covered employer is fulfilling its obligations under the employer mandate to provide health insurance to its employees and dependents that is affordable and provides minimum value. It is titled "Applicable Section 4980H Safe Harbor" because the IRS asks employers to indicate through use of code letters which safe harbor it has used to determine affordability (see pages 21–25 above on safe harbors) or, alternatively, other reasons why the employer is not liable for an inadequate-coverage penalty. The form asks for information on a monthly basis because the IRS evaluates compliance with the employer mandate on a monthly basis and will impose penalties on a monthly basis.

Completing Part II

On the left hand side of the page, along the same line that says "**Part II Employee Offer and Coverage**," Form 1095-C asks for "**Plan Start Month** (Enter 2-digit number)." The IRS seeks information here about the month in which the health plan year begins. If it is a calendar year plan, the employer would enter "01" for January. If it is a typical fiscal year plan, the employer would enter "07" for July. If the plan year begins in October, the employer would enter "10." Employers who have more than 50 FTEs and are covered by the employer mandate, but who nevertheless do not offer health insurance coverage, should enter "00."

Line 14 asks the employer with respect to the individual employee whether it offered the employee and any dependents health coverage each calendar month of the year. To fulfill the employer mandate for a calendar month, coverage must be offered for every day of that month. In most cases, for any given month, if an employee has received an offer of coverage or has actually enrolled in the employer's plan, this requirement will be satisfied. Resignations or terminations that become effective on something other than the first or last day of a month mean that the employee in question has not been offered coverage for that month.

Each of **lines 14, 15, and 16** makes use of nine different indicator codes for reporting the various kinds of answers an employer might have for each question depending on the facts about each employee.

For **line 14**, employers must use Code Series 1, which is set out at the end of this section. It may also be found in the IRS Instructions for Forms 1094-C and 1095-C for any given year.

An employer who made an offer of coverage to an employee for all 12 months of the year (or who made no offer of coverage to an employee in any months of the year) will enter the appropriate Code Series 1 indicator code in **the box marked "All 12 Months" on line 14**. Where an employee has received an offer of coverage for some but not all 12 months, the employer should report either the kind of offer made or that no offer was made in each of the boxes corresponding to the individual months of the year. Employers must fill in an indicator code for each month even if the employee was not a full-time employee for some of those months.

For local government employers, the most commonly used indicator codes for line 14 are likely to be the following.

- **1A.** A qualifying offer of coverage was made to the employee and all of his or her dependents, if any. A qualifying offer is an offer of minimum essential coverage (MEC) that provides minimum value (note that any employer-sponsored policy will offer MEC because ACA provisions applicable to health insurer issuers require that they offer MEC). The employee's contribution for self-only coverage must be equal to or less than 9.5% (as adjusted annually) of the mainland single federal poverty line or qualify as affordable under one of the ACA's safe-harbor provisions (see pages 22–25).
- **1H.** The employer made no offer of coverage to the employee or offered coverage that was not minimum essential coverage (for

example, vision and dental coverage or medical coverage that does not include hospitalization). Employers *with fully insured health plans* will use this indicator code for employees hired during the course of the year for those months during which they were either not employees or were in a limited non-assessment period.

- **1G.** *Self-insured employers* will use this indicator code for employees who have received an offer of coverage for at least one month of the year and were either (1) part-time employees for some part of the calendar year or (2) hired during the course of the year, for those months during which they were not full-time, were not employees, or were in a limited non-assessment period.

Using the Qualifying Offer Method on Form 1095-C

When an employer enters indicator code 1A on **line 14**, it is using the Qualifying Offer Method of reporting. Under the Qualifying Offer Method, instead of reporting the lowest-cost monthly premium paid by the employee for self-only coverage on **line 15**, the employer enters the indicator code 1A on **line 14** of Form 1095-C and leaves **line 15** blank. The employer should enter indicator code 1A for each month it made a qualifying offer to the employee. For some employees this will be for all 12 months; for others, it may be for fewer than 12 months. If an employee has received a qualifying offer only for the months of July through December, for example, the employer should enter indicator code 1A on **line 14** for each of those months and leave **line 15** blank. For the months of January through June, for which the employee did not receive a qualifying offer (as in the case of a variable-hour or new employee), the employer should enter the appropriate offer indicator code on **line 14** and enter the dollar amount of the lowest-cost employee-only monthly premium for that month on **line 15**.

An employer using indicator code 1A on line 14 does not need to fill in **line 15**. An employer will need to report on line 15 only if it has entered indicator code 1B, 1C, 1D, 1E, 1J, or 1K for an employee for any month (or all months) on line 14. Indicator codes 1B, 1C, 1D, 1E, 1J, and 1K report that offers of minimum essential coverage (MEC) were made to the employee only; the employee and dependents; the employee and spouse; or the employee, spouse, and dependents, but that coverage, although providing minimum value, was not affordable.

If an employer has entered indicator codes 1B, 1C, 1D, 1E, 1J, or 1K on line 14, it must now enter on line 15 the amount of the *employee-only share* of the lowest-cost monthly premium for self-only coverage that provides minimum value—that is, the cost for employee coverage reported by indicator codes 1B, 1C, 1D, 1E, 1J, and 1K on line 14. Some local government employers offer employee-only coverage without any cost to the employee. If that is the case, the employer should enter "0.00" in either the "All 12 Months" column or for those months for which the offer was made (these will be the same months for which indicator codes 1B, 1C, 1D, 1E, 1J, and 1K was entered on line 14). If the employer leaves the boxes on line 15 blank because the employer paid the entire cost of the employee-only premium, the form will be considered incomplete—the employer must enter "0.00." Otherwise, employers should enter the employee's share of the employee-only premium on a monthly basis on line 15.

Even if a local government employer pays the entire cost of employee-only premiums, an individual employee may still be making health insurance premium payments. The employee may have elected to enroll in a higher-tier plan offering increased coverage at a higher price. Or the employee may have chosen dependent or spouse and dependent coverage. That information is *not* reported on line 15. The only thing that gets reported is the amount the employee's share of the *lowest cost, employee-only* premium would be if that is what the employee had elected. And that is only if indicator code 1B, 1C, 1D, 1E, 1J, or 1K was entered on line 14.

In **line 16**, employers are to enter whichever of the **Code Series 2** indicator codes is applicable to the individual employee who is the subject of the Form 1095-C. Code Series 2 may be found below or in the IRS Instructions for Forms 1094-C and 1095-C for a given year.

Code Series 2 covers a number of different circumstances. The Code Series 2 indicator codes local government employers are most likely to use are the following.

- **2A.** The individual was *not* an employee on *any* day of that month. Use this code for the months before a new employee starts and for any month in which a terminated employee is covered by the employer's plan through COBRA continuation coverage.
- **2B.** This indicator code will be used in several different circumstances. Enter "2B" if the individual was not a full-time employee (averaging less than 30 hours of service per week) and did not receive an offer of coverage. Enter "2B" if the individual was not a full-time employee, but received an offer of coverage anyway

and did not enroll in minimum essential coverage. Enter "2B" if the employee's coverage or offer of coverage ended before the last day of the month because the employee was terminated and he or she declined the offer of COBRA continuation coverage.

- **2C.** Use this indicator code when an employee has been enrolled in coverage every day of that month. If an employee has been enrolled in coverage every day of each month of the year, enter "2C" in the box for "All 12 Months." *This indicator code trumps any other applicable indicator code and should be used whenever it applies, except where the employee has been terminated and is enrolled in COBRA continuation coverage.* For terminated employees enrolled in COBRA continuation coverage, use indicator code 2A.
- **2D.** Enter indicator code "2D" for any month during which an employee is in a limited non-assessment period. This includes variable-hour employees during their initial measurement period.[2]

Completing Part III, Lines 17 and Following

Only employers with self-insured plans should fill out Part III. Employers with fully insured plans do not need to provide the information in Part III because their insurers will report that information to the IRS.

Lines 17–34 of Form 1095-C provide spaces for a self-insured employer to enter information about other members of the employee's family who are enrolled in coverage through the employer's self-insured plan. For spouses or dependents who have been enrolled in employer coverage for all 12 months, the employer should enter an "X" or a check mark in **column (d)** ("Covered all 12 months"). If a spouse or dependent has been enrolled in the employer's plan for less than the entire year, the employer should indicate those months during which the person was enrolled for all of the days of that month.

---

2. A limited non-assessment period is a period during which an employee is not counted for the purposes of assessing the no-coverage and inadequate-coverage penalties, whether or not the employee is offered health insurance. Initial measurement periods, waiting periods, or initial months of employment are examples of limited non-assessment periods. For the purposes of reporting on Forms 1094-C and 1095-C, an employee in a limited non-assessment period is not considered a full-time employee during that period. For more on limited non-assessment periods, see page 84 above.

Conditional Offers of Spousal or Dependent Coverage

When an offer of coverage to a spouse is subject to one or more objective conditions, an employer may treat the spouse as having received an offer of coverage whether or not the spouse actually met the conditions. Examples of objective conditions include that the spouse not be covered or eligible for Medicare or that the spouse not be eligible for health insurance through his or her own employer. If the spouse were offered conditional coverage and satisfied the conditions, the spouse could be eligible for a premium tax credit depending on his or her financial circumstances. If the spouse were offered conditional coverage, but did not satisfy the conditions because he or she was eligible for coverage elsewhere, the spouse would not be eligible for a premium tax credit to purchase the employer's health coverage. In either case, the employer would not be subject to a no-coverage or inadequate-coverage penalty because employers are not required to offer spousal coverage. So employers are allowed to report conditional offers to spouses as offers of coverage.

In contrast, when an offer of coverage to dependents is subject to one or more conditions, an employer may *not* treat the dependents as having received an offer of coverage unless the employer knows an employee's dependents meet the conditions of the offer. That is because employers are required to offer dependent coverage.

Indicator Code Series 1 for Use on Line 14 of Form 1095-C

1A. Minimum essential coverage providing minimum value offered to full-time employee with the employee contribution for self-only coverage equal to or less than 9.5% of the single federal poverty line and at least minimum essential coverage offered to spouse and dependent(s) (qualifying offer). This code may be used to report for specific months for which a qualifying offer was made, even if the employee did not receive a qualifying offer for all 12 months of the calendar year.

1B. Minimum essential coverage providing minimum value offered to employee only.

1C. Minimum essential coverage providing minimum value offered to employee and at least minimum essential coverage offered to dependent(s) (but not to spouse).

1D. Minimum essential coverage providing minimum value offered to employee and at least minimum essential coverage offered to spouse (but not to dependent(s)). If the offer of coverage to a spouse was valid only if the spouse satisfied certain conditions, do not use code 1D. Instead use code 1J.

1E. Minimum essential coverage providing minimum value offered to employee and at least minimum essential coverage offered to dependent(s) and spouse. If the offer of coverage to a spouse was valid only if the spouse satisfied certain conditions, do not use code 1E. Instead use code 1K.

1F. Minimum essential coverage *not* providing minimum value offered to employee; employee and spouse or dependent(s); or employee, spouse, and dependents.

1G. Offer of coverage to an individual who was not an employee for one or more months of the calendar year or to an employee who was a part-time employee (and may not have been an employee for one or more months in the calendar year) and who enrolled in self-insured coverage for one or more months of the calendar year.

1H. No offer of coverage (employee not offered any health coverage or employee offered coverage that is not minimum essential coverage, which may include one or more months in which the individual was not an employee).

1I. Reserved for future use by IRS.

1J. Minimum essential coverage providing minimum value offered to employee and at least minimum essential coverage conditionally offered to spouse; minimum essential coverage not offered to dependent(s).

1K. Minimum essential coverage providing minimum value offered to employee, at least minimum essential coverage offered to dependents, and at least minimum essential coverage conditionally offered to spouse. (See Conditional Offers of Spousal or Dependent Coverage above, for additional information about conditional offers.)

Indicator Code Series 2 for Use on Line 16 of Form 1095-C

2A. The employee was not employed on any day of the calendar month. Do not use code 2A for a month if the individual was an employee of the employer on one or more days of the calendar month but not all. Do not use code 2A for the month during which an employee terminates employment unless the employee is enrolled in COBRA continuation coverage.

2B. The employee is not a full-time employee for the month and did not enroll in minimum essential coverage, if offered for the month. Also enter code 2B if the employee is a full-time employee for the month and whose offer of coverage (or coverage, if the employee was enrolled) ended before the last day of the month solely because the employee terminated employment during the month (so that the offer of coverage would have continued if the employee had not terminated employment during the month).

2C. Used for any month in which the employee enrolled in health coverage offered by the employer for each day of the month, regardless of whether any other code in Code Series 2 (other than code 2E) might also apply (for example, code 2F for a Section 4980H affordability safe harbor). Do not enter 2C if code 1G is entered in the All 12 Months box in line 14 because the employee was not a full-time employee for one or more months of the calendar year. Do not enter code 2C for any month in which a terminated employee is enrolled in COBRA continuation coverage (enter code 2A).

2D. Used for any month during which an employee is in a limited non-assessment period for Section 4980H(b). If an employee is in an initial measurement period, enter code 2D (employee in a Section 4980H(b) Limited Non-assessment Period) for the month, and not code 2B (employee not a full-time employee).

2E. Used for any month for which the multi-employer arrangement interim guidance applies for that employee, regardless of whether any other code in Code Series 2 (including code 2C) might also apply. This relief is described under Offer of Health Coverage in the Definitions section of the IRS Instructions for Forms 1094-C and 1095-C. This code number applies only to multi-employer plans that have been collectively bargained.

2F. If the employer used the Section 4980H Form W-2 safe harbor to determine affordability for this employee for the year, enter code 2F. If an employer uses this safe harbor for an employee, it must be used for all months of the calendar year for which the employee is offered health coverage.

2G. If the employer used the Section 4980H federal poverty line safe harbor to determine affordability for this employee for any month(s), enter code 2G.

2H. If the employer used the Section 4980H rate of pay safe harbor to determine affordability for this employee for any month(s), enter code 2H.

2I. Reserved for future use by the IRS.

Forms 1094-B and 1095-B: Information Required of Self-Insured Employers Only

Overview of Forms 1094-B and 1095-B

The "B" series of ACA reporting forms are required of any issuer of health insurance plans providing minimum essential coverage (MEC). Employers offering health coverage through fully insured plans are sponsors, but not issuers, of health insurance. They have no responsibility to file Forms 1094-B and 1095-B. The health insurers with whom they have contracted will send Form 1095-B to their employees and copies (along with Form 1094-B, a transmittal cover sheet) to the IRS. But employers offering health coverage through self-insured plans are both sponsors *and* issuers of health insurance. Self-insured employers are therefore required to provide both employees and the IRS with the substantive information solicited on Form 1095-B. These employers must fill out one Form 1095-B for each employee who has enrolled in health coverage. Because Form 1095-B is designed to give the IRS information about which individuals are getting insurance through which health plan so that it may determine compliance with the *individual* mandate, Form 1095-B does not require information about employees who were offered but did not enroll in health coverage or who were not offered coverage.

Self-insured employers who have 50 or more full-time equivalent employees therefore have dual reporting requirements. As issuers of health insurance coverage, they must report information related to the individual mandate on Form 1095-B and as employers sponsoring health coverage, they must report information related to the employer mandate on Form 1095-C. To simplify reporting for self-insured employers, the IRS allows them to report the information requested on Form 1095-B in Part III of Form 1095-C instead.

Do any employers have to file both Forms 1094-B and 1095-B? The answer is "yes." Small employers not covered by the ACA's employer mandate do not have to file Forms 1094-C and 1095-C since they cannot be subject to penalties for failure to provide coverage. But if a small employer offers health coverage and is self-insured, it must file Form 1094-B and 1095-B in its role as *issuer* of health insurance. Small employers who offer health coverage through a fully insured plan have no reporting responsibilities at all.

Table 1.   Reporting obligations and forms for employers, based on employer size and plan type

Number of full-time employees	Fully insured plan	Self-insured plan
100 or more: Subject to reporting and penalties	Form 1095-C, Parts I and II only for each employee who was a full-time employee for at least one month of the calendar year; insurer will file Form **1095-B**	Form 1095-C, Parts I and II for each employee who was a full-time employee for at least one month of the calendar year; Part III for any employee enrolled in coverage
50–100: Subject to reporting and penalties	Form 1095-C, Parts I and II only for each employee who was a full-time employee for at least one month of the calendar year; insurer will file Form 1095-B	Form 1095-C, Parts I, II, and III for each employee who was a full-time employee for at least one month of the calendar year; Part III for any employee enrolled in coverage
Fewer than 50: Will never be subject to no-coverage or inadequate-coverage penalties, but offers of coverage must be reported	Employer does not file; insurer will file **1095-B**	Employer files Form **1095-B**

Line-by-Line Description: Form 1094-B

Form 1094-B is the transmittal form, or cover sheet, for a self-insured small employer's batch of Forms 1095-B. It is entirely self-explanatory, asking for the issuing employer's name and employer identification number, address, the name and telephone number of a contact person, and the total number of Forms 1095-B being submitted with the Form 1094-B transmittal sheet.

Line-by-Line Description: Form 1095-B

One Form 1095-B must be completed for each employee enrolled in the employer's self-insured plan. **Line 1** asks for the name of the "Responsible Individual." Enter the name of the enrolled employee in this box. The term "responsible individual" is used with health insurers in mind and refers to the individual insured who would receive this statement from the insurer. In the case of self-insured employers, however, the employer is the insurer and the individual insured is the employee, so the "responsible individual" is the employee.

Lines 2–7 are self-explanatory.

In **line 8**, an employer should enter code "B" for "employer-sponsored coverage."

Line 9 should be left blank.

Employers should leave **Part II, lines 10–15**, blank, notwithstanding the fact that the section is titled "Employer Sponsored Coverage." Most of the organizations filling out Form 1095-B will be insurance companies. They will be reporting the name of the employer with whom they have contracted to provide the health coverage. A self-insured employer does not need to complete this section.

The employer will identify itself in **Part III**, "Issuer or Other Coverage Provider," in **lines 16–22**. The employer is the "issuer or other coverage provider" by virtue of being self-insured. The information requested is self-explanatory.

In **Part IV, lines 23–28**, the employer will enter information about the employee identified in line 1 and any spouse and dependents covered with that employee. **Columns (a), (b), and (c)** ask for identifying information— name, Social Security number, and date of birth if a Social Security number is not available.[3] An employer should check the box in **column (d)**, "Covered all 12 months," if the person identified in that line was covered *at least one day* of *every month* of the year being reported.

If the individual was not covered for at least one day of every month, the employer should indicate in **column (e)** which months the employee was covered for at least one day by checking the box for that month.

---

3. The IRS permits employers to truncate employee Social Security numbers on the forms given to the employees themselves by using asterisks (*) or the letter X for the first five numbers of the Social Security number and providing the correct last four numbers. The forms provided to the IRS, however, must have the full Social Security number.

Reporting COBRA Continuation Coverage

Consider the case of a full-time employee who has been offered minimum essential coverage (MEC) and who has been participating in the employer's health plan. That employee may become ineligible to continue participating in the health plan by ceasing to be a full-time employee. That can happen in either of two ways. First, the employee's employment may end altogether. Second, the employee's hours may be reduced so that this person is no longer a full-time employee and thus no longer eligible to participate in the health plan according to the terms of the plan. In either case, the person is likely to be eligible to continued health insurance coverage for a period of time under The Consolidated Omnibus Budget Reconciliation Act (COBRA), as will the person's spouse and dependents.

How is the employer to report the offer of coverage information for individuals in these circumstances?

Termination of Employment

Where an individual is no longer eligible to participate in the employer's health plan because employment has ended, a counter-intuitive situation arises. The employer must make COBRA continuation coverage available to the former employee and any spouse or dependents that have also been covered under the employer's plan. COBRA coverage is at the employee's own expense. The former employee and his or her family members may accept or decline the offer of COBRA coverage. But, according to the IRS instructions for Form 1095-C, the offer of COBRA coverage is recorded on line 14 using Code 1H (meaning "no offer of coverage"). So, despite the fact that COBRA coverage is offered, the IRS is told that no offer of coverage was made to the former employee under the employer's health plan.

On line 16, for the month in which employment ended, the employee should either be coded as 2C if employment ended on the last day of the month or 2B if employment terminated before the last day of the month. For those months of the year after the month of termination, the former employee is coded on line 16 as 2A, indicating that he or she is not an employee.

For the months of the year before the employment was terminated, the employer reports the offer of coverage in the regular course of things—on line 14, it indicates that the employee was offered coverage (using Code

1A or 1E or whatever is appropriate) and on line 16, that the employee was employed full-time (using Code 2C in all likelihood).

Reduction of Hours

Where the individual is no longer eligible to participate in the employer's health plan because his or her hours of work have been reduced, the employer reports the offer of coverage for all the months the employee was actively employed full time. For the months during which COBRA was offered after the employee was reduced to less than full time, the employer reports the offer of coverage using Code 1E, regardless of whether the employee accepts the COBRA coverage. Code 1E ("minimum essential coverage providing minimum value offered to employee; employee and spouse or dependent(s); or employee, spouse and dependents") is used instead of Code 1A because the qualifying offer of coverage code is only used with respect to full-time employees. How the employer will report the employee's part-time status on line 16 will depend on whether the employee is in a limited non-assessment period. Part-time employees are reported using Code 2B. Employees in a limited non-assessment period are reported using Code 2D.

Variable-Hour Employees, Loss of Coverage under the Look-Back Measurement Period, and COBRA

Consider the following hypothetical.

The City of Paradise uses the look-back method for determining the health coverage eligibility of its variable-hour employees. During her initial measurement period, Linda is deemed to be a full-time employee and is offered coverage for the following stability period. During the next measurement period, the city determines Linda is not full-time. The city withdraws its offer of coverage for the next stability period. Linda continues working. Must the city offer Linda COBRA coverage? The answer is "yes." An employee may continue to work and be covered by COBRA continuation coverage.

Reporting about Retirees

The rules regarding reporting of health insurance arrangements that benefit retirees depend in large part on whether the retiree is eligible for Medicare—that is, whether the retiree is 65 years of age or older.

Retirees 65 and Older

Medicare and Medicare Advantage plans provide, for purposes of the Affordable Care Act, minimum essential coverage for individuals age 65 and older. So virtually all retirees that age have, by definition, minimum essential coverage through Medicare.

An IRS rule provides that reporting is not required under the ACA for an individual's minimum essential coverage offered by an employer if the individual is covered by other minimum essential coverage for which reporting is required.[4] Reporting is required for Medicare and Medicare Advantage plan participants.[5] Therefore, an employer need not report at all on offers of coverage it makes to retirees that is supplemental in some way to Medicare. The reporting that Medicare does covers all reporting that is required. This means that retiree-only health reimbursement arrangements (HRAs) offered to Medicare-eligible retirees to assist in the purchase of a Medigap policy, to pay Part B premiums, or to purchase medical supplies not covered by Medicare do not need to be reported.[6]

Retirees under 65

For retirees under 65, Medicare does not apply, so there is no Medicare reporting for those individuals. Therefore employers are not automatically relieved of their obligation to report to the IRS.

Employers offering retiree health coverage through fully insured plans (that is, plans offered under an insurance contract with an insurance carrier) will not have any reporting requirements for their retirees, except in the year an employee retires. For fully insured plans, the provider of minimum essential coverage is the health insurance company, and it is the health insurance company that will report the coverage, through Forms 1094-B and 1095-B. Employers do not generally have to report offers of coverage to retirees on

---

4. *See* 26 C.F.R. § 1.6055-1(d)(2).
5. *See* 26 C.F.R. § 1.6055-1(c)(3)(2).
6. *See* 26 C.F.R. § 1.6055-1(d)(2)(ii).

Forms 1094-C and 1095-C. *In the year that an employee retires, however,* and only in that year, the employer will enter the appropriate codes on lines 14 and 16 of Form 1095-C for those months preceding retirement and will enter Code 1H ("no offer of coverage") on line 14 and Code 2A ("not an employee") on line 16 for any month in which the employer made an offer of retiree coverage.[7]

If, on the other hand, the plan is self-insured by the employer, then the employer is the issuer, or provider, of minimum essential coverage. It therefore reports the coverage on Forms 1094-B and 1095-B each year it provides the retiree coverage. As with a fully insured plan, an employer does not need to report offers of coverage to retirees on the C forms except in the year of retirement.[8]

Retiree-Only Health Reimbursement Arrangements

As discussed in Part 4, a health reimbursement arrangement (HRA) is a tax-favored, employer-sponsored plan through which retirees (as well as current employees) may be reimbursed for qualified medical expenses. HRAs are funded solely by employer contributions. The money that accumulates in an HRA may be carried over from year to year and funds contributed to the account in one year may be used to reimburse expenses incurred in a later year. Funds may never be used for anything but qualified medical expenses, as defined by the IRS. Qualified medical expenses include health insurance premiums, co-payments and co-insurance, and deductibles.[9] Under the ACA, HRAs can be used as a stand-alone plan for retiree benefits without the retirees having to be enrolled in a group health plan, because a retiree-only plan is considered an excepted benefit and is therefore not subject to ACA requirements.[10] For this reason, retiree-only HRAs have become an increasingly attractive way for local government employers to fund retiree health benefits.

---

7. *See* Internal Revenue Service, Instructions for Forms 1094-C and 1095-C for the applicable reporting year.

8. *See* 26 C.F.R. § 1.6055-1(c)(2).

9. *See* 26 U.S.C. § 213(d).

10. Like HRAs for current employees, however, retiree-only HRAs must allow participants to waive their rights to their account balances on a yearly basis. *See* pages 73–74 above.

Although a retiree-only HRA is not subject to the market reforms applicable to other health plans (see above, pages 6–12), under the ACA it is considered a form of self-insured minimum essential coverage (MEC) and will have to be reported by employers on Forms 1094-B and 1095-B. Employers of all sizes offering retiree-only HRAs will have to report, as this requirement is applicable to them in their role as health insurers rather than as employers. Employers will not have to file the C forms because retirees are not employees.

Section 4980H Transition Relief for Non-calendar Year Plans for 2016 Only

Recognizing that non-calendar year plans would have some special challenges in preparing for ACA reporting, the IRS provided for transition relief for non-calendar year plans for the 2015 reporting year. It has extended that relief on a very limited basis for the 2016 reporting year for those months of an employer's 2015 plan year that fell in calendar year 2016. The relief for reporting year 2016 is referred to as "Section 4980H Transition Relief" on line 22 in box C and lines 23–35, column (e), of Form 1094-C.

There are four different forms of transition relief for non-calendar year plans for 2016. The first is for an employer with fewer than 100 full-time employees or 100 full-time equivalent employees (FTEs). The IRS refers to this as "50–99 Transition Relief." The second is for employers with more than 100 full-time employees or 100 FTEs. The IRS refers to this as "100 or More Transition Relief." The third form of transition relief is available to employers who have offered coverage to at least 70% of their full-time employees during those months of the 2016 calendar year that fall within the 2015 plan year. The final form of relief is for employers with non-calendar year plans who did not extend coverage to dependents during the 2015 plan year but have taken steps to do so going forward.

50–99 Transition Relief

This form of transition relief allows an employer who qualified for non-calendar year plan transition relief for the 2015 reporting year to treat any employee (and any dependents) as having been offered coverage for those months in 2016 that were part of the 2015 plan year.[11] To be eligible for this form of transition relief, an employer

- must have had 50–99 employees or FTEs on business days in 2014,
- during the period February 9, 2014, through December 1, 2014, must not have reduced the size of its workforce or reduced the overall hours of service of employees in order to qualify for transition relief, and
- as of the last day of the 2015 plan year, must not have eliminated or materially changed the health coverage it offered as of February 9, 2014.

Thus, in Part III, lines 23–35, column (a), of Form 1094-C, the employer offering a non-calendar year plan may indicate that the employee and dependents, if any, were offered coverage for all of the months of the year. The employer will be assessed neither a no-coverage penalty nor an inadequate-coverage penalty for its employees for the months in 2016 that were part of its 2015 plan year. In column (e) of lines 23–35, which is titled "Section 4980H," the employer should enter code "A" to indicate that it is claiming 50–99 Transition Relief.

100 or More Transition Relief

This second form of 2016 transition relief offers more limited relief than does 50–99 Transition Relief. To be eligible for this form of transition relief, an employer must

- have had 100 or more employees or FTEs on business days in 2014,
- have had a non-calendar year plan in 2015, *and*
- *be subject to a no-coverage penalty for any month in 2016 that falls within the 2015 plan year.*

---

11. To be eligible for 2015 non-calendar year plan transition relief, an employer with 50–99 employees would have had to have (1) offered affordable, minimum value coverage to an employee no later than the first day of the 2015 plan year and (2) offered coverage in accordance with the plan's eligibility requirements as they existed on February 9, 2014 (in other words, the plan could not have become more restrictive with respect to which employees are eligible to enroll). The employee would have had to have been eligible to participate in the plan as of December 27, 2012 (or later if hired later).

The relief in this case is a lesser penalty than the employer would otherwise face for its failure to offer coverage to 95% of its employees during the 2016 plan year.

As discussed above in Part 1, employers who fail to offer any health insurance coverage at all to their employees (and their dependents), or who fail to offer coverage to more than 5% of their full-time employees (and their dependents), will be liable for the no-coverage penalty if at least one of those employees not offered coverage receives a premium tax credit from the IRS to assist in the purchase of Exchange-based health insurance. The penalty will be calculated for 2016 by multiplying 1/12 of $2,160 (or $180) times the number of full-time employees the employer has for that month (excluding employees in a limited non-assessment period; see page 84).[12]

Normally, the number of employees an employer has for any month may be reduced by 30 for the purpose of calculating the no-coverage penalty. The 100 or More Transition Relief allows an employer with a non-calendar year plan to reduce the number of employees that it has for those months that fall within the 2015 plan year by 80 for the purpose of calculating the no-coverage penalty.

Consider the following example.

> *Paradise County has a non-calendar year plan that runs from July 1 through June 30 of the following year. Therefore, its 2015 plan year began on July 1, 2015, and ended on June 30, 2016. The 2016 plan year began on July 1, 2016. Paradise County should have offered coverage to 225 employees, but in fact offered coverage to only 150 during each month of 2016. For the months of July–December 2016, the months in the 2016 plan year, the no-coverage penalty the county owes will be calculated using the standard reduction of 30 in the number of county employees. It will be liable for a penalty of $35,100 each month. That figure is reached by multiplying 1/12 of $2,160 (or $180) by 195 employees (225 full-time employees minus 30).*
>
> *Because of transition relief, the penalty will be less for the months of January–June 2016, which were part of the 2015 plan year. For these months, the county will calculate the no-coverage penalty using*

---

12. In 2015, the monthly no-coverage benchmark penalty was 1/12 of $2,000, but the ACA provides that the $2,000 figure be increased each year.

the transition relief reduction of 80 in the number of county employees. Thus, Paradise County will be liable for a penalty of $26,100 for each month of that period. That figure is reached by multiplying 1/12 of $2,160 (or $180) by 145 employees (225 full-time employees minus 80).

Non-calendar Year Plan 70% Transition Relief for 2016

An employer who has offered a non-calendar year plan for the 2015 plan year, and offered coverage to at least 70% of its full-time employees and their dependents during those months of the 2015 plan year that fall in 2016 (for example, during January–June 2016 if the plan year runs from July 1, 2015–June 30, 2016), may report itself as having offered minimum essential coverage to 95% of its employees for those months of the 2015 plan year that fall in 2016. The employer does so by entering an "X" in the Yes box in column (a) of Form 1094-C, lines 23–35, for the applicable months in 2016. An employer who meets these requirements for relief will not be assessed a no-coverage penalty for those months of the 2015 plan year that fall in 2016, even if one or more employees receives a premium tax credit from the IRS.

Non-calendar Year Plan Dependent Coverage Transition Relief for 2016

Employers with non-calendar year plans who offered health coverage to their employees, but not to some or all of their employees' dependents, may be eligible for relief from the no-coverage and inadequate-coverage penalties for 2016. This relief is available with respect to employees not offered dependent coverage for the 2013, 2014, and 2015 plan years, provided that the employer can show that it has taken steps during the 2015 plan year to extend coverage to dependents up to age 26 in future plan years. In this case, an employer may treat the offer of coverage to an employee as an offer of coverage to the employee and any dependents for those months of 2016 that fall within the 2015 plan year. The employer does so by entering an "X" in the Yes box in column (a) of Form 1094-C, lines 23-35, for the applicable months in 2016. An employer who meets these requirements for relief will not be assessed a no-coverage penalty for those months of the 2015 plan year that fall in 2016, even if one or more employees receives a premium tax credit from the IRS. *Employers availing themselves of this form of transition relief may not report using the Qualifying Offer Method in 2016.* This is because use of the Qualifying Offer Method requires that minimum essential coverage (MEC) that is affordable and provides minimum value was offered to an employee and his or her dependents and spouse for all months of the calendar year. In this case, there was no actual offer of coverage to dependents during the months of 2016 that fall within the 2015 plan year.

A Warning Applicable to All Four Forms of 2016 Transition Relief for Non-calendar Year Plans

Employers with non-calendar year plans must still accurately report the terms of the coverage actually offered to each employee for each month on Form 1095-C (the individual form that goes to each employee and to the IRS) so that the IRS may determine whether an employee qualifies for a premium tax credit. An employee may qualify for a premium tax credit for those months in 2016 that are part of the 2015 plan year even though the employer will not be assessed a no-coverage penalty or will be assessed a lesser penalty by virtue of the transition relief.

Providing Form 1095-C to Employees and Filing the Forms with the IRS

The IRS has established deadlines by which employers must give information about their health care coverage to employees and file information returns with the IRS. These deadlines parallel the deadlines by which employers must file tax return information about their employees with the IRS.

Reporting to Employees

Form 1095-C (or Form 1095-B for self-insured small employers) must be given to employees by January 31 of the year following the reporting year. For example, employers reporting the health insurance coverage they have offered employees in 2016 have until January 31, 2017, to give a Form 1095-C to each employee. In years where January 31 falls on a Saturday or Sunday, the deadline is the next business day following January 31.

Forms may be given to employees electronically if they specifically consent to this manner of communication. See the introductory pages of the IRS Instructions for Forms 1094-C and 1095-C. Otherwise, the forms should be sent by mail or hand-delivered.

Reporting to the IRS

Hard-copy paper returns must be filed with the IRS on or before February 28 of the year following the reporting year. The deadline is extended to March 31 if the employer files electronically. Employers who must file 250 or more copies of a form are required to file electronically.

An employer filing electronically must test-file before the deadline to ensure that its computer system and software meet IRS technical specifications.[13]

Extensions of Time

Extensions of the time in which to file may be requested for Sections 6055 and 6056 returns as for any other return in accordance with the rules set forth in I.R.C. Section 6081 and 26 C.F.R. Sections 6081-1 and 6081-8.

Small Employers with Self-Insured Plans

If an employer with fewer than 50 employees sponsors a self-insured health plan, it must file Forms 1094-B and 1094-C (pursuant to I.R.C. Section 6055), even though it is not subject to the employer mandate (see pages 81–82). This is because the purpose of Forms 1094-B and 1094-C is, in part, to give the IRS information necessary to evaluate whether individuals are complying with the individual mandate. Local government employers who provide health insurance through a multi-employer trust are considered self-insured. Employers must give Form 1095-B returns to participants in its health plan by January 31 of the following year and file Form 1094-B and 1095-B returns with the IRS by February 28 (March 31 if filing electronically).

Substitute Forms

Employers can substitute their own forms for IRS Forms 1094-B and 1095-B, 1094-C and 1095-C if they so choose, but they must meet the requirements set forth in IRS Publication 5223, *General Rules and Specifications for Affordable Care Act Substitute Forms 1095-A, 1094-B, 1095-B, 1094-C, and 1095-C*. For most employers, this is not advised.

---

13. For detailed information on the IRS Affordable Care Act Information Returns (AIR) program, see https://www.irs.gov/for-Tax-Pros/Software-Developers/Information-Returns/Affordable-Care-Act-Information-Return-AIR-Program.

Alternate Method of Reporting to Employees for Employers Eligible to Use the Qualifying Offer Method

Only fully insured employers who check box A (Qualifying Offer Method) on line 22 of Form 1094-C are eligible to use the alternate reporting method. The alternate reporting method may only be used for employees who received an offer of coverage. Regardless of whether an employer uses the alternate reporting method or issues a Form 1095-C to an employee, *the employer must still file a Form 1095-C for that employee with the IRS.* Because a Form 1095-C must still be prepared, the value of this alternate method is unclear.

Employers may use the alternate method of reporting for employees who received a qualifying offer *for all twelve months* of the year *but declined coverage.* Use of the alternate method is not required. Employers must issue a Form 1095-C to any employee who received a qualifying offer for some, but not all 12, months of the year, whether or not that employee accepted coverage, and to all employees who received a qualifying offer for all twelve months and enrolled in coverage.

An employer using the alternate method gives the employee a statement in lieu of Form 1095-C. The statement must contain

1. the employer's name, address, and employer identification number (EIN);
2. the name and telephone number of an employer representative whom the employee may contact to receive information about the offer of coverage and about the information the employer will file on the IRS copy of Form 1095-C;
3. a declaration that the employee and any qualifying dependents received a qualifying offer for all 12 months of the calendar year and are *not*, therefore, eligible for a premium tax credit; and
4. an instruction to the employee to consult IRS Publication 974, *Premium Tax Credit,* for more information on the premium tax credit.[14]

---

14. *See* Internal Revenue Service, Instructions for Forms 1094-C and 1095-C for the applicable tax year.

Penalties for Failure to File

In addition to the no-coverage and inadequate-coverage penalties discussed beginning on page 33, there are penalties for failure to file the required reports. The penalty for failure to file a required 1094 or 1095 return is $250 per day for each return or statement that is *missing, late, or incomplete.*[15] In other words, an employer with 50 employees would be liable for $12,500 per day for failure to give its employees their Form 1095-C statements and another $250 per day for failure to file its 1094-C transmittal form with the IRS.

Self-insured small employers not covered by the ACA must furnish Form 1095-B to its employees and the Form 1094-B transmittal sheet and all copies of Forms 1095-B to the IRS. A self-insured small employer with 35 employees, for example, would be liable for $8,750 per day for failure to provide Form 1095-B to employees and another $250 per day for failing to file Form 1094-B with the IRS.

There is a total annual maximum penalty of $3,000,000.

---

15. *See* 26 C.F.R. §§ 301.6056-1(i)(1) and (2) and 26 U.S.C. § 6721(a) for Section 6056 (Forms 1095) reporting and 26 C.F.R. §§ 1.6055-1(h)(1) and (2) and 26 U.S.C. § 6722(a) for Section 6055 (Forms 1094) reporting. The fines were increased from their previous levels in the Trade Preferences Extension Act of 2015. These penalties also apply to failure to file or late filing of income tax informational returns to the IRS and the failure to issue or late issuance of Forms W-2 and 1099 to employees and independent contractors.

Definitions

applicable large employer (ALE). Any employer who has employed an average of 50 or more *full-time equivalent* employees during the preceding calendar year. In this book, an "applicable large employer" is referred to as a "covered employer." See below.

covered employers. Employers who have an average 50 or more full-time employees. They are sometimes referred to as *applicable large employers* or "ALEs."

covered employer self-funded plan reporting exception. Allows covered employers who would normally have to provide plan participants a copy of Form 1095-B (in their role as plan issuers) along with a copy of Form 1095-C (in their role as employers) to provide the information required by Form 1095-B in Part III of Form 1095-C. Small employers not covered by the ACA's employer mandate who have self-funded plans cannot take advantage of this exception and must file Form 1095-B information on Form 1095-B itself.

eligible employer-sponsored plan. Group health insurance coverage for employees under an insured plan, a grandfathered plan offered in a group market, or a self-insured plan for employees.

full-time employee. An employee who works an average of at least 30 hours per week in any given calendar month.

full-time equivalent employee (FTE). A combination of employees, each of whom individually does not qualify as a full-time employee because he or she does not work an average of least 30 hours per week, but who in combination are counted as the equivalent of a full-time employee solely for the purposes of determining whether an employer is an applicable large employer.

Form 1095-B. The form on which issuers of health insurance coverage report the names of employees covered by employer-sponsored group health plans to employee participants and to the IRS to allow it to enforce the individual mandate.

Form 1094-B. The summary transmittal form which accompanies the *Forms 1095-B* submitted by health insurance issuers, including small employers who are not covered by the ACA but who offer health insurance through a self-funded plan that is a multi-employer trust.

Form 1095-C. The form on which employers covered by the ACA report offers of coverage to employees and to the IRS to allow it to enforce the employer mandate. Covered employers who offer health insurance through a fully insured plan must issue a Form 1095-C for each employee who received an offer of health insurance coverage for at least one month of the year. Self-insured covered employers may use Form 1095-C to report their Form 1094-C information at the same time and streamline their reporting.

Form 1094-C. The summary transmittal form which accompanies the *Forms 1095-C* submitted by employers to the IRS.

Internal Revenue Code § 6055 (26 U.S.C. § 6055). Requires health insurance companies who issue plans and self-insured employers to provide individual statements to individuals they cover stating whether the company or employer provided *minimum essential coverage* satisfying the individual mandate. The reporting to individuals is done on IRS *Forms 1095-B*, copies of which are submitted to the IRS with IRS *Form 1094-B*, which is a transmittal cover sheet that aggregates the information contained in the Forms 1095-B.

Internal Revenue Code § 6056 (26 U.S.C. § 6056). Requires *covered employers* (called *applicable large employers* or *ALEs* under the ACA) to provide individual statements to every person who was a *full-time employee* for at least one month of the preceding calendar year showing whether that employee, spouse, or any dependents were offered health insurance and, if so, the amount of the lowest cost, employee-only premium. If the employer has offered group health insurance coverage to part-time employees, the employer must also furnish this statement to those part-time employees who enrolled in the coverage. The reporting to individuals is done on IRS *Forms 1095-C*, copies of which are submitted to the IRS with IRS *Form 1094-C*, which is a transmittal cover sheet that aggregates the information contained in the Forms 1095-C.

limited non-assessment period. A period during which an employee is not counted for the purposes of assessing the no-coverage and the inadequate-coverage penalties. For the purposes of reporting on *Forms 1094-C* and *1095-C*, an employee in a limited non-assessment period is not considered a full-time employee during that period.

minimum essential coverage (MEC). Coverage that satisfies an individual's obligation to have health insurance coverage under the individual mandate. For the purpose of *Forms 1094* and *1095* reporting, the IRS states that "minimum essential coverage" refers to health coverage under an *eligible employer-sponsored plan*.

minimum value. For an employer to avoid the inadequate-coverage penalty, it must offer *minimum essential coverage* that is affordable and provides "minimum value." In general, a plan provides minimum value if it covers at least 60% of the total allowed costs of benefits that could be expected to be incurred under the plan if the plan applied to a statistically standard population. The Department of Health and Human Services and the Internal Revenue Service have provided a minimum value calculator. (To download the minimum value calculator, Google "aca minimum value calculator" and click on the XLS link for the cms.gov website.) To determine whether a plan provides minimum value, an employer would enter certain information into the calculator, such as deductibles and co-pays. The calculator applies the data related to the statistically standard population and determines whether the plan provides minimum value.

In reality, this calculation may be beyond the capacity of individual employers to make. Employers may have to rely on brokers to ensure that the plans offered by the employer do in fact provide minimum value, but employers will have to report to the IRS that their plans provide minimum value and make that statement to employees.

qualifying offer. An offer of *minimum essential coverage* that provides *minimum value* made to a full-time employee for whom a no-coverage or inadequate-coverage penalty could apply. The employee cost for employee-only coverage cannot exceed 9.5% (as adjusted annually) of the federal poverty line for single persons divided by 12, and must provide that the offer includes an offer of minimum essential coverage to the employee's spouse and dependents.

variable-hour employee. An employee whose hours of service cannot reasonably be determined on the employee's start date.

Appendix 1

Form 1094-C

Form 1094-C

Department of the Treasury
Internal Revenue Service

Transmittal of Employer-Provided Health Insurance Offer and Coverage Information Returns

▶ Information about Form 1094-C and its separate instructions is at *www.irs.gov/form1094c*

☐ CORRECTED

OMB No. 1545-2251

2016

Part I Applicable Large Employer Member (ALE Member)

1 Name of ALE Member (Employer)

2 Employer identification number (EIN)

3 Street address (including room or suite no.)

4 City or town

5 State or province

6 Country and ZIP or foreign postal code

7 Name of person to contact

8 Contact telephone number

9 Name of Designated Government Entity (only if applicable)

LEAVE BLANK

10 Employer identification number (EIN)

LEAVE BLANK

11 Street address (including room or suite no.)

LEAVE BLANK

12 City or town

LEAVE BLANK

13 State or province

LEAVE BLANK

14 Country and ZIP or foreign postal code

LEAVE BLANK

15 Name of person to contact

LEAVE BLANK

16 Contact telephone number

LEAVE BLANK

17 Reserved .

For Official Use Only

18 Total number of Forms 1095-C submitted with this transmittal . . . . ▶

19 Is this the authoritative transmittal for this ALE Member? If "Yes," check the box and continue. If "No," see instructions . . ▶

Part II ALE Member Information

20 Total number of Forms 1095-C filed by and/or on behalf of ALE Member . . . . ▶

21 Is ALE Member a member of an Aggregated ALE Group? . . . . ☐ Yes ☒ No

Local government employers answer no.

If "No," do not complete Part IV.

22 Certifications of Eligibility (select all that apply):

☐ **A.** Qualifying Offer Method ☐ **B.** Reserved ☐ **C.** Section 4980H Transition Relief ☐ **D.** 98% Offer Method

Under penalties of perjury, I declare that I have examined this return and accompanying documents, and to the best of my knowledge and belief, they are true, correct, and complete.

▶ _____ Signature   _____ Title   _____ Date

For Privacy Act and Paperwork Reduction Act Notice, see separate instructions.   Cat. No. 61571A   Form **1094-C** (2016)

Fill out lines 20–22 only on the Authoritative Transmittal.

Part III ALE Member Information—Monthly

Coverage to 95% of full-time employees and dependents?

Do not count employees in a limited non-assessment period in responding to columns (a) and (b).

	(a) Minimum Essential Coverage Offer Indicator		(b) Section 4980H Full-Time Employee Count for ALE Member	(c) Total Employee Count for ALE Member	(d) Aggregated Group Indicator	(e) Section 4980H Transition Relief Indicator
	Yes	**No**				
			Employers certifying eligibility for 98% Offer reporting do not have to fill out column (b).	Include full-time, part-time, and employees in a limited non-assessment period.	not applicable	Use indicator code: • A if claiming 2016 transition relief for employers with 50–99 FTEs. • B if claiming 2016 transition relief for employers with 100 or more FTEs. • A or B should appear in either the "All 12 Months" box or the box for any applicable months in column (e).
23 All 12 Months	☒	☐				
24 Jan	☐	☐			☐	
25 Feb	☐	☐			☐	
26 Mar	☐	☐			☐	
27 Apr	☐	☐			☐	
28 May	☐	☐			☐	
29 June	☐	☐			☐	
30 July	☐	☐			☐	
31 Aug	☐	☐			☐	
32 Sept	☐	☐			☐	
33 Oct	☐	☐			☐	
34 Nov	☐	☐			☐	
35 Dec	☐	☐			☐	

DO NOT COMPLETE THIS PART

Part IV   Other ALE Members of Aggregated ALE Group

Enter the names and EINs of Other ALE Members of the Aggregated ALE Group (who were members at any time during the calendar year).

	Name	EIN		Name	EIN
36			51		
37			52		
38			53		
39			54		
40			55		
41			56		
42			57		
43			58		
44			59		
45			60		
46			61		
47			62		
48			63		
49			64		
50			65		

Appendix 2

Form 1095-C

600117

Form **1095-C**
Department of the Treasury
Internal Revenue Service

☐ VOID
☐ CORRECTED

OMB No. 1545-2251
2016

Employer-Provided Health Insurance Offer and Coverage
▶ Do not attach to your tax return. Keep for your records.
▶ Information about Form 1095-C and its separate instructions is at www.irs.gov/form1095c.

EMPLOYEE INFORMATION

EMPLOYER INFORMATION

Part I Employee

1 Name of employee

2 Social security number (SSN)

3 Street address (including apartment no.)

4 City or town

5 State or province

6 Country and ZIP or foreign postal code

Applicable Large Employer Member (Employer)

7 Name of employer

8 Employer identification number (EIN)

9 Street address (including room or suite no.)

10 Contact telephone number

11 City or town

12 State or province

13 Country and ZIP or foreign postal code

Part II Employee Offer of Coverage   Plan Start Month (Enter 2-digit number): _____

	All 12 Months	Jan	Feb	Mar	Apr	May	June	July	Aug	Sept	Oct	Nov	Dec
14 Offer of Coverage (enter required code)		1H	1H	1H	1A	1A	1A	1A	1A	1A	1A	1A	1A
15 Employee Required Contribution (see instructions)	$	$	$	$	$	$	$	$	$	$	$	$	$
16 Section 4980H Safe Harbor and Other Relief (enter code, if applicable)													

Part III Covered Individuals   If Employer provided self-insured coverage, check the box and enter the information for each individual enrolled in coverage, including the employee. ☐

(a) Name of covered individual(s)	(b) SSN or other TIN	(c) DOB (If SSN or other TIN is not available)	(d) Covered all 12 months	(e) Months of Coverage											
				Jan	Feb	Mar	Apr	May	June	July	Aug	Sept	Oct	Nov	Dec
17			☐	☐	☐	☐	☐	☐	☐	☐	☐	☐	☐	☐	☐
18			☐	☐	☐	☐	☐	☐	☐	☐	☐	☐	☐	☐	☐
19			☐	☐	☐	☐	☐	☐	☐	☐	☐	☐	☐	☐	☐
20			☐	☐	☐	☐	☐	☐	☐	☐	☐	☐	☐	☐	☐
21			☐	☐	☐	☐	☐	☐	☐	☐	☐	☐	☐	☐	☐
22			☐	☐	☐	☐	☐	☐	☐	☐	☐	☐	☐	☐	☐

Indicator Codes for line 14 are on pages 97–98. The codes in the boxes are examples only.

▶ **14**

▶ **15**

▶ **16**

Never enter anything in line 15 when you are using Code 1A.

1095-C

Form 1095-C
Department of the Treasury
Internal Revenue Service

Employer-Provided Health Insurance Offer and Coverage
▶ Do not attach to your tax return. Keep for your records.
▶ Information about Form 1095-C and its separate instructions is at *www.irs.gov/form1095c*

☐ VOID
☐ CORRECTED

OMB No. 1545-2251

2016

Part I Employee

1 Name of employee
Jennifer Johnson

2 Social security number (SSN)
555-55-5555

3 Street address (including apartment no.)
723 Tar Heel Drive

4 City or town
Paradise

5 State or province
N.C.

6 Country and ZIP or foreign postal code
12345

Applicable Large Employer Member (Employer)

7 Name of employer
City of Paradise, North Carolina

8 Employer identification number (EIN)
00-0000000

9 Street address (including room or suite no.)
987 Awesome Street

10 Contact telephone number
555-555-5555

11 City or town
Paradise

12 State or province
N.C.

13 Country and ZIP or foreign postal code
12345

Part II Employee Offer of Coverage

Plan Start Month (Enter 2-digit number): _____

	All 12 Months	Jan	Feb	Mar	Apr	May	June	July	Aug	Sept	Oct	Nov	Dec
14 Offer of Coverage (enter required code)	1A												
15 Employee Required Contribution (see instructions)	$	$	$	$	$	$	$	$	$	$	$	$	$
16 Section 4980H Safe Harbor and Other Relief (enter code, if applicable)													

14

15

16

Fill in line 15 only if you have entered 1B, 1C, 1D, 1E, 1J, or 1K on line 14 in the box for "All 12 Months" or for any individual month.

Part III Covered Individuals

If Employer provided self-insured coverage, check the box and enter the information for each individual enrolled in coverage, including the employee. ☐

(a) Name of covered individual(s)	(b) SSN or other TIN	(c) DOB (If SSN or other TIN is not available)	(d) Covered all 12 months	(e) Months of Coverage											
				Jan	Feb	Mar	Apr	May	June	July	Aug	Sept	Oct	Nov	Dec
17			☐	☐	☐	☐	☐	☐	☐	☐	☐	☐	☐	☐	☐
18			☐	☐	☐	☐	☐	☐	☐	☐	☐	☐	☐	☐	☐
19			☐	☐	☐	☐	☐	☐	☐	☐	☐	☐	☐	☐	☐
20			☐	☐	☐	☐	☐	☐	☐	☐	☐	☐	☐	☐	☐
21			☐	☐	☐	☐	☐	☐	☐	☐	☐	☐	☐	☐	☐
22			☐	☐	☐	☐	☐	☐	☐	☐	☐	☐	☐	☐	☐

For Privacy Act and Paperwork Reduction Act Notice, see separate instructions.

Cat. No. 60705M

Form **1095-C** (2016)

600117

Form **1095-C**

Department of the Treasury
Internal Revenue Service

Employer-Provided Health Insurance Offer and Coverage

▶ Do not attach to your tax return. Keep for your records.

▶ Information about Form 1095-C and its separate instructions is at *www.irs.gov/form1095c*

☐ VOID
☐ CORRECTED

OMB No. 1545-2251

2016

Part I Employee

1 Name of employee Jennifer Johnson	2 Social security number (SSN) 555-55-5555
3 Street address (including apartment no.) 723 Tar Heel Drive	
4 City or town Paradise	5 State or province N.C.	6 Country and ZIP or foreign postal code 12345

Applicable Large Employer Member (Employer)

7 Name of employer City of Paradise, North Carolina	8 Employer identification number (EIN) 00-0000000
9 Street address (including room or suite no.) 987 Awesome Street	10 Contact telephone number 555-555-5555
11 City or town Paradise	12 State or province N.C.	13 Country and ZIP or foreign postal code 12345

Part II Employee Offer of Coverage

Plan Start Month (Enter 2-digit number): _____

	All 12 Months	Jan	Feb	Mar	Apr	May	June	July	Aug	Sept	Oct	Nov	Dec
14 Offer of Coverage (enter required code)	1A												
15 Employee Required Contribution (see instructions)	$	$	$	$	$	$	$	$	$	$	$	$	$
16 Section 4980H Safe Harbor and Other Relief (enter code, if applicable)													

Part III Covered Individuals If Employer provided self-insured coverage, check the box and enter the information for each individual enrolled in coverage, including the employee. ☐

(a) Name of covered individual(s)	(b) SSN or other TIN	(c) DOB (if SSN or other TIN is not available)	(d) Covered all 12 months	(e) Months of Coverage											
				Jan	Feb	Mar	Apr	May	June	July	Aug	Sept	Oct	Nov	Dec
17 William Johnson	888-88-8888			☐	☐	☐	☐	☐	☒	☒	☒	☒	☒	☒	☒
18 Susan Johnson	333-33-3333		☒												
19 William Johnson, Jr.		10/31/16		☐	☐	☐	☐	☐	☐	☐	☐	☐	☒	☒	☒
20				☐	☐	☐	☐	☐	☐	☐	☐	☐	☐	☐	☐
21				☐	☐	☐	☐	☐	☐	☐	☐	☐	☐	☐	☐
22				☐	☐	☐	☐	☐	☐	☐	☐	☐	☐	☐	☐

▶ 14
▶ 15
▶ 16

Only self-insured employers fill in Part III. Insurers provide Part III information for employers with fully insured plans.

For Privacy Act and Paperwork Reduction Act Notice, see separate instructions.   Cat. No. 60705M   Form **1095-C** (2016)

Appendix 3

Form 1094-B

110116

Form **1094-B**

Department of the Treasury
Internal Revenue Service

Transmittal of Health Coverage Information Returns

▶ Information about Form 1094-B and its separate instructions is at *www.irs.gov/form1094b*.

OMB No. 1545-2252

2016

1 Filer's name

2 Employer identification number (EIN)

3 Name of person to contact

4 Contact telephone number

5 Street address (including room or suite no.)

7 State or province

8 Country and ZIP or foreign postal code

9 Total number of Forms 1095-B submitted with this transmittal . . . . ▲

Under penalties of perjury, I declare that I have examined this return and accompanying documents, and to the best of my knowledge and belief, they are true, correct, and complete.

▲ Signature

Title

▲ Date

For Official Use Only

☐☐☐☐☐☐
☐☐

For Privacy Act and Paperwork Reduction Act Notice, see separate instructions.   Cat. No. 61570P   Form **1094-B** (2016)

Appendix 4

Form 1095-B

560116

Form **1095-B**

Department of the Treasury
Internal Revenue Service

☐ VOID

☐ CORRECTED

OMB No. 1545-2252

20**16**

Do not attach to your tax return. Keep for your records.

▶ Information about Form 1095-B and its separate instructions is at www.irs.gov/form1095b.

Part I Responsible Individual

1 Name of responsible individual	2 Social security number (SSN or other TIN)	3 Date of birth (If SSN or other TIN is not available)
Sally Mployee	222-22-2222	

4 Street address (including apartment no.)	5 City or town	6 State or province	7 Country and ZIP or foreign postal code
891 Valley Street	Paradise Heights	North Carolina	12345

8 Enter letter identifying Origin of the Health Coverage (see instructions for codes): · · · ▶ ☐

9 Reserved

Part II Information about Certain Employer-Sponsored Coverage (see instructions)

10 Employer name	11 Employer identification number (EIN)

12 Street address (including room or suite no.)	13 City or town	14 State or province	15 Country and ZIP or foreign postal code

Part III Issuer or Other Coverage Provider (see instructions)

16 Name	17 Employer identification number (EIN)	18 Contact telephone number
Paradise County, North Carolina	11-0000000	(919) 555-6666

19 Street address (including room or suite no.)	20 City or town	21 State or province	22 Country and ZIP or foreign postal code
246 Main Street	Paradise	N.C.	12345

Part IV Covered Individuals (Enter the information for each covered individual.)

(a) Name of covered individual(s)	(b) SSN or other TIN	(c) DOB (If SSN or other TIN is not available)	(d) Covered all 12 months	(e) Months of coverage											
				Jan	Feb	Mar	Apr	May	Jun	Jul	Aug	Sep	Oct	Nov	Dec
23 Sally Mployee	222-22-2222		☒												
24 Roy Spousie	888-88-8888		☐							☒	☒	☒	☒	☒	☒
25															
26															
27															
28															

1095-B (2016)

This means the employee.

No employer should fill out Part II.

Self-insured small employers fill out Parts III and IV.

Mark "X" if employee was covered for at least one day for all 12 months or in each month, as applicable.